The Looking Glass

Walter Farrell, O.P.

READING FOR ETERNITY

Paluch Publications
Chicago

Imprimi potest:
    Eduardus L. Hughes, O.P., S.T.Lr., Prior Provincialis

Nihil obstat:
    Joannes L. Callahan, O.P., S.T.Lr., Ph.D.
    Guillelmus B. Mahoney, O.P., S.T.Lr., Ph.D.

Imprimatur:
  ✠ Samuel Cardinal Stritch
    Archbishop of Chicago
    April 21, 1951

Walter Farrell, O.P.
is also the author of
"A Companion to the Summa"
Four Volumes
published by Sheed and Ward, New York

"Essence of the Natural Law"
St. Dominic's Press, Ditchling, Sussex, England

PALUCH PUBLICATIONS
Published by the J. S. Paluch Co., Inc.
P. O. Box Number 3386   Chicago 54, Illinois

CONTENTS

CHAPTER ONE

Beauty in Action

A BEAUTY may be living or dead. But not all dead beauties have been handed over to the undertaker, though they must maintain the immobility of a corpse. There are, for example, the women whose beauty is shattered by a smile, the women who dare not walk lest they sag or slouch, who smash the fragile illusion of beauty by their softest word. The possessors, in a word, of a static beauty, a cold, inhuman, dead thing which is no more than an angle, an aspect of beauty, the photographer's illusion. It is a beauty consistent with posing but not with living. Such beauty is never to be found in a kitchen or bending over a wash-tub; but is rather to be looked for on the cover of a magazine or in the window of a dress shop. Fittingly the dummies of a display window wear a look of hopeless resignation or a sad smile which becomes more ghastly the longer a window-gazer fixes his eyes on it. It is no fun to be perpetually dead, even though one is beautifully dead.

There are other beauties in which movement is not a destruction but a revelation of beauty. These are they who inspired Chesterton's good wish, which was also a prayer: "As on a stairway, go in grace." A smile, a wave of the hand, the unconscious perfection flashed in bending over to catch a whispered word, are the sparkles of different facets of a jewel beyond price. This beauty is a living beauty which finds its perfection in movement, in life.

For all that, it is a mysterious thing. The athlete catches something of it, though holding it in contempt, in his search for economy of movement; while, paradoxically, the woman searching for the smooth texture of grace comes, startled, upon the proficiency of the athlete. For these two are not to be separated. One or the other may be disregarded or despised: when one is had, the other is inevitably present.

As a physical thing this has been analyzed and studied in an age that does not neglect physical beauty. Sometimes it has been solemnly classed as muscular coordination, more vaguely as symmetry, or even, musically, as rhythm; and parallels have been found in the instinctive lightness of foot, speed, power, and economy of motion in the animal world.

We could know there was something wrong with this analysis even though we did not suspect that woman was not just another animal. For we readily recognize the ominous, the sinister in a woman who walks with the smooth stealth of a cat, the lithe deadliness of a tiger, or the cold, slithering brilliance of a snake. Ominous and sinister do not enter into the make-up of woman. There is the added detail, of no little moment, that women the country over are spending hours learning to walk, to talk, to smile, and to sit in ways that will not startle beauty into flight; while not a cat, tiger, or snake gives it all a moment's thought. For an instinctive thing, it takes a great deal of labor and patience in a woman.

There is a more than a cheerful note of superiority in the fact that women can learn these things. There is a revelation contained here. Evidently, then, there is a right way and a wrong way, a beautiful as well as an ugly way of doing these things. Nor is there reason for discouragement, after the long months of exercises and concentration that have bent all the physical powers to the command of reason into a smooth coordination, in the discovery of some savage who possesses all this grace and beauty of action without a moment of practice. This merely brings out the truth that much of the physical education in beauty is a process of unlearning the bad habits, the wrong ways of doing very ordinary things. There is a human way of doing these things, common alike to savage and debutante. The human way can be ignored, semicultivated or wholly embraced by either one.

Therein lies a sharp differentiation from the animal world. There is a human beauty of action, a beauty that can be rejected or maintained, that can degenerate or progress. Coordination by instinct, symmetry in action can be found in the animals; but not a deliberate harmonious control of faculties ordered to one common end. That is the human mark, the mark of reason's control, the mark of the sovereign which is stamped on all the royal appurtenances, even on such details as clothes, furnishings, words, a gesture. It is the brilliant splendor of the form breaking through the matter as the brilliance of the sun penetrates the inert mass of a cloud to clothe the cloud with robes of golden glory.

A child may stroll out of the house on a beautiful May morning with one stocking on and one off, totally unembarrassed, but a woman in the same predicament has legitimate title to her confusion. This is an action that escaped the control of her reason, a thing she did not mean to do at all; the fruit of worry, absent-mindedness, of distraction, or one of those enemies of rationality that take the soul out of a human action and leave it a dead, inhuman, stupid thing. Reason is the soul of human action, the form that brings life to it; as that life is fuller, more vigorous, the order of reason shines more brilliantly through the material of the action. It is smoother, more graceful, more economically proficient, because to it are bent the human energies under the control of reason to an end that belongs to reason. It has a fuller beauty.

All this is in the physical order. As such it is a symbol of a deeper, more vital, more independent—because more human—beauty of human action. Beauty is not to be limited to a pose, an angle, an aspect; it is not static but vital. Neither is it to be limited to a space of ten or twenty years, to a class that escapes the penalties of physical labor, to the educated, the wealthy, to a nation, a race. And the reason for this declaration of beauty's independence is to be found in its source: the splendor of reason's order breaking through into a human life. That soul of human acts does not weary, year by year, its steps do not grow sluggish, its face fall, all the light go out of its eyes. Rather it becomes fuller, richer, amassing more treasures with the passing years.

To put this truth more plainly, this exclusively human beauty of action belongs as properly to the actions of the street begger as to the glamor girl of the day. The joyous, enveloping smile of the girl-mother bending over her divine Infant in the crude cradle of Bethlehem was not more beautiful than the agonized love on the face of that tired, middle-aged mother standing beneath the cross on which her Son was dying so slowly. Infants and dying men are not given to raptures on beauty; but that unsympathetic, bloodthirsty mob on Calvary saw more of the splendor of Mary's soul than did Joseph in Bethlehem, despite all the power of penetration given him by his love for his wife.

It is not chance or accident that explains the artists of the ages passing over the beauties of Caesar's court to paint again and again the picture of the luxurious outcast of society kneeling at the foot of the cross to wash the feet of Christ once more with her tears. Rather the explanation is to be found in art's sure instinct for beauty. The saddest meal in the world was eaten on Holy Thursday in an upper room in Jerusalem; but its beauty could be caught but vaguely by a master in his greatest work.

This is beauty as man alone can possess it. This is human, indeed superhuman, beauty, as superior to mere physical beauty of movement in its vitality, its independence, its splendor, as that physical beauty of action is superior to the beauty of pose, of an angle. It is not the static thing of a statue, not the momentary thing of a photograph, not the temporary things of a few years; but a living, flowing grace that stretches the length of a lifetime in its eagerness to taste of eternity. Co-ordination, symmetry, yes; but more than that, it is the harmonious ordering of the appetites of man to a common end worthy of the being who alone is master of his action.

It is odd that we should stop at the sign of human beauty. We do not ordinarily stop at the gate that bears the name of our friends, and go home satisfied that we have called on them.

The neon sign of a restaurant does not satisfy the appetite sharpened to a razor-edge by hunger. Signs are messengers that push through the otherwise inviolable gates of our minds with invitations that no stretch of the imagination can mistake for the party to which they give us entry. But the signs of beauty seem to be an exception; they are such beautiful things that we stand wrapped in admiration at their perfection, forgetting that they are only signs.

Dead or static beauty is a sign and a promise of dynamic, living beauty, though the promise is not always kept. Living beauty of physical movement is a sign of a still higher, still more exclusively human beauty of action. We shall never satisfy our hunger for beauty by looking at its signs. We shall not only never possess beauty, we shall never appreciate it until the sign is recognized as a sign and beauty seen as beauty.

A statue can be beautiful or ugly, a movement graceful or awkward, and a human action can be perfectly proportioned, alive with inner beauty, or it can be deformed, dead, a thing of horror. In each case the difference is between a brilliant, sunny day that makes a cloudless sky seem infinitely distant and mysteriously deep, and a dark night that makes of the sky a menace so close as to seem a sack dropped over our heads. In each case it is the difference of the brilliant splendor of humanity shining through or smothered; but progressively in each case the darkness is deeper and the ugliness more pronounced because the capacity for beauty is so much greater.

In the rush of everyday life we cannot carry about with us a valise full of philosophic definitions and analysis; the measure of beauty and ugliness must be compressed into a tiny container without bulk, for, of course, we must use it continually since we must continually confront ugliness and beauty. It might have been put into a locket in the form of contrasting pictures of the Lady Mary and some other woman who had learned too late the emptiness of another way of life. Actually, the norm has been crowded into two small words: virtue and sin.

To say that virtue is beauty in action is not to grasp at far-fetched metaphors. To damn sin as ugliness is not to descend to name-calling. We are not being vaguely poetic when we recognize beauty in Christ's welcome to children. For the one is eminently human, the other has little of humanity about it; and an act is beautiful or ugly as it irradiates that brilliance of reason's order which is the mark of humanity. Virtue is a human thing, supernatural virtue, even somewhat of a divine thing; while sin is a deformed human act, hiding its ugliness in secrecy.

The special horror of this ugliness of sin was emphasized in Christ's eager love for the sinner, a love that was compassionate, merciful; and, when its help was refused, wistful. We might find a parallel in the emotions of a man who has just seen a beautiful woman throw acid on her face. Sin is such a wanton destruction of peerless beauty. Christ wanted to help the sinner immediately, to do something, anything, even hang on a Cross, that something might be done. Because He was God, Christ could and did do more than wring His hands. He could do what was impossible to mere men:—restore that beauty where its restoration was desired.

Beauty does come hard. Particularly that exclusive human beauty which is utterly independent and exhaustless in its vitality. Virtue comes hard. It, too, demands exercise and diet, with many a pessimistic glance into the mirror; but here the hopelessness of the purpose for beauty is denied, not by vanity, but by faith and courage. And then, after months and years of effort, we come upon that beauty full-fledged in the actions of a child who has seemingly made no effort.

CHAPTER TWO

Family Likeness

THERE COMES a time in every human life when the crayons must be put away. The practice period is over, and we get down to the business of living, for now our actions are our own. We stand before the blank canvas of life and sketch in the picture that will make us or break us. A firm, skillful stroke, a sure eye, and a sense of proportion are important: but with all these, the result can be a sorry failure if we work from the wrong model.

The model upon which our eyes are fixed makes a tremendous difference in the living of human life; in fact, it makes all the difference. This is apparent if we change the figure and see the actions, by which we live that life, as motions to a goal. It is rare indeed that a flyer receives acclamations for flying the wrong way; nor are medals cast for those who only go part way, or who do not get under way at all. The important thing in motion is the goal and the reaching of it.

From its beginning, action takes on the likeness of its goal with the ready adaptability of a child reflecting the emotions of the mother into whose face he is looking. Let her smile, and he answers with a joyous grin; let her be stern, and he trembles; let her weep, and his heart is sad. So with our actions. Let them be aimed at ugliness, and they lose all beauty; let their goals be stupid, frivolous, narrow, mean, and the actions give back an unholy reflection of these same qualities. The object or end is the sire of the action; never can the family likeness be denied.

It is not by chance that we have so closely related the high and the heroic; the high goals are what adorn the actions of man with the splendor of heroism. In fact, stopping short of heroism, we may make it a general rule that the height of a goal determines the beauty of the action. For the ear to drink in the ordered harmony of a symphony is a higher thing than to suffer the disordered din of traffic; for the heart of a woman to be fixed on a child, than to have pushed all else out of its narrow confines to make room for a consuming passion for bridge. The solitaire or puzzle addict may keep himself out of mischief, drugging his mind with this anesthetic, but his activity is a lowly thing compared to the relentless pursuit of truth by a scholar.

The fact is that men are marksmen, and the projectile they hurl is life itself. It will be thrown at something or other, high or low, pathetic or comic. If man hurls it at himself, he has taken on the fruitless task of ridding himself of a boomerang; if he aims it beneath himself into the animal world, his life has the pathetic incongruity of Brussels lace delicately draped over a refuse can; if it is cast at vague generalities, popular targets of the day, his life has the emptiness of a starving man dreaming of banquets.

What is true of the life of man is true of each of his faculties, of each of the principles of his motion; indeed the goal of man's life is always the goal upon which his mind fixes its eye and to which his heart rushes or plods.

The trouble is that in the world there are no goals high enough for the mind and heart of a man. Paradoxically, when the mind and heart are made to satisfy themselves with goals that are not high enough, every human goal is found to be too high and there is a rush back to the child's game of skipping rope, away from the fearsome hurdles of life. Only when the eye is fixed on the goal too high for any man of himself, can the hurdles of natural life be taken in stride.

In a word, to give his actions the splendor of high goals, man must have long vision, a vision that takes in the far boundaries of the universe and sweeps on to the limitless horizons of divinity. He needs a preview of heaven if he is to see the world; if he looks only at the latter, he is blind even to what he thinks he sees. That preview of heaven is usually called faith.

It would have been well worth living before the age of gangster movies and jitterbugs to have seen the expression on the faces of the audience of Christ when He said: "Amen I say to you, if you have faith as a grain of mustard seed, you shall say to this mountain, remove from hence hither, and it shall remove." Faith has always been an astounding thing; nonchalance can never be the mark of one who is seeing through the eyes of God. In fact, so astounding is it that it sometimes seems better to transform it into something quite normal and human to save ourselves the shock of its truth.

At no time in the history of the world has that process of substituting a human double for divine faith gone farther than in our own time. Faith has been described in terms of a "religious sense," a vague feeling, as comforting and intangible as the sense of well-being that follows on a good dinner. It has been paraded under the disguise of a smug assurance of personal salvation that makes mediocrity comfortable and human life a long unruffled glide into heaven. Men have thought to produce it by a mechanical hypnotism that left them possessed by "religion" and obliterated the worries of the past. No wonder its enemies have come to look on faith as a substitute offered to the weak-minded or weak-kneed who could not think or were afraid of the consequence of thought!

The Catholic woman swaying from a strap in a subway train or clutching desperately for support on a jolting bus, knows very well that her faith is not a matter of her disposition, her digestion, or the comfort of her feet. Its possession does not mark the end of struggle; rather it sets up high, hard goals that make every instant of life a challenge to tireless battle. She gets as tired and battered as any of her contemporaries yet she hugs firmly to her breast faith's challenge to still more struggle. Of all her contemporaries, she alone sees faith for what it is, and guards it jealously.

Her faith is not a substitute for reason, it is a perfection thereof; it is an intellectual virtue whose object is truth, indeed the first and supreme Truth from which all that is true has its truth. It would have been no light thing for a daughter of Eve to be the confidant of God, to hear the ineffable whispers of unspeakable things, even though it meant no more than the trust and love that confidence always implies. But these truths of faith, the inner secrets of divinity, the intimacies of the family life of God, the mysteriously eternal activity of the Three Persons within and without Themselves are not merely confidences. They are not the result of a divine heart in need of consolation, of a divine soul too full to contain itself, of a love that shares without creating, and badly in need of support and nourishment. These truths of the first Truth are all given to the humblest woman *for a divine fruition*. Since they hold out the promise of the eternal future of humankind, they are not to be admired, but reached for. In a word, they are the high targets worthy of the marksman who is man, toward which he can hurl his life with all the reckless gallantry of a love that reaches out not merely above humanity, but beyond the ends of the earth, beyond the remote confines of the universe.

It is true that faith touches on more than the first Truth, God Himself. It embraces the consoling details of the humanity of Christ: the helplessness of His infancy, the fatigue of His journeys, the patient simplicity of His words, the love of His heart, the fatigue of His soul and the bitter loneliness of His death. Faith takes in all the precious lessons of Holy Scripture and tradition, all the solemn definitions of the Church: the Annunciation, the birth of the Virgin's Son, the rebirth of man by baptism, the resurrection of penance, the companionship of Christ's presence in the Eucharist. But in all these things faith has not moved a step from its first object, the supreme Truth which man is destined to enjoy for eternity; it reaches out to whatever else is of faith only to the extent that this other thing has an order to that divine fruition, that it leads men along the sharp, narrow path at the end of which is divinity.

CHAPTER THREE

Living Room

OR MANY years men have known the Shenandoah valley. They have journeyed through it and have been struck by its beauty; or they have lived there, and that beauty has sunk into their blood and bones. Men have studied that valley from all sides, lovingly, as a woman turns a jewel about in her fingers to relish the sparkle of its beauty; they have climbed the mountains on one side or the other and reveled in the miles added to their vision. It was not until recently that airplanes swept down the middle of the valley, making an exquisite miniature of it for the hungry eye to devour all its beauty in one greedy glance. That aerial view did not destroy the truth and beauty seen by the dweller on the floor of the valley, or falsify the perspective of the mountaineer peering down from the heights of the Blue Ridge; the Trail of the Lonesome Pine was not destroyed by the path of the sky-sleeper. Rather, the plane opened to the eyes and minds of men new visions, larger horizons, more encompassing beauties.

With the eye of reason, we see just so far and no farther: as far as the walls of the universe. Faith does not destroy the truths that reason uncovers, nor does it absolve man from the use of his reason. It is not a substitute for reason, but a vision perfecting the mind of man to see beyond the walls of the universe into the depths of divinity, to look back on the world in which he lives, as from a great height that gives him a "God's eye-view" of the little and the great things that make up the world in which men and women work out their lives.

Faith is a view, a superior view opening up truths that only God could know. In itself faith perfects the mind of man far beyond anything else that can come to it in the universe. Yet for all that, faith is an imperfect thing. Although the vision of God should be spread before us, we have not the eyes of God. We are soaring in the heights, but we have not the eagle's power to take in the details of the panorama that unfolds beneath us. We are looking at truths too bright for our eyes, so we move in obscurity. Faith *is* obscure. By faith a man moves through darkness; but he moves securely, his hand in the hand of God. He is literally seeing through the eyes of God, as a blind man sees through the eyes of his friend, because all that he believes, he believes precisely by reason of the word of the First Truth. The darkness of faith is not a discouragement, a ground for distrust; it is a promise of that time when we shall no longer see "as in a glass, darkly, but face to face." It is a challenge to those who would "become as little children," a challenge that can be met only by bending the stiff neck of pride while we listen again to the wise words of a Father as He tells us things our puny experience can never reach.

What a petty world it would be could we know all about it; what a clumsy, limited set of blueprints would hold its design if their every detail could be crowded into the stumbling minds that we boast of! What a bedraggled divinity would God be if proud men could have their way and search out His last secret with the instruments of their wisdom! The limitations of the human mind, so sharply pointed out by faith, are not an embarrassment; they are a comfort. In moments of self-honesty, we have seen those limitations, and greater ones, standing out starkly before us. We have known too well that not by our knowledge can a universe, or even a single human life, be ordered. At the moment we realized how important it was that there be someone who knows more than man can ever know, indeed who knows all things.

Love and hope need a long road, a secure road, a high goal; they need faith. Not a wishful faith that depends on the constancy of man or even on the stability of the universe; rather it must be an infallable, a divine faith, a solid bedrock on which their feet can stand firmly as they strike their lusty blows in the battle of life. It took great love to stand on Calvary beneath the cross; it took tremendous faith to come down from Calvary and continue life. Mary, from her earliest beginnings, was going not to Bethlehem alone, nor to Nazareth alone, not even to Calvary alone, but to God; that goal shone before her eyes as did the star before the wise men's eyes on their long road from the east.

Moreover, faith brings the comfort of security in the midst of an uncertain world. A woman who has been given the gift of faith stands in the middle of her life somewhat as the pioneers stood in the center of their newly completed stockade; for this gift of faith bars the entrance of the enemy falsehood much more surely than ever did the stockade keep out the Indians. In the emptiness of darkness the stained-glass windows of Notre Dame are no more than a part of that universal blackness; with the morning sun streaming through them they are a blaze of gorgeous color that stops the heart in its beating. Light is the medium by which color is seen. Thus the First Truth is the medium by which men believe; there is no more possibility of falsehood calling that supernatural belief into life than there is of darkness bringing out the glory of color in a stained-glass window. All the smallest details that fall under faith do so only so far as they have an order to God, to the First Truth. To include truth under falsehood is no more possible than to include being under nothing, or goodness under evil. It is not only the *thing* that faith believes but the *very reason* for belief which excludes the possibility of falsehood undermining the foundations which faith gives to man's life. Such is the security of faith.

It was no wonder Christ could talk of faith tossing mountains into the sea much as a boy might toss pebbles into a pond. That is child's play for faith, a trifle compared to the power given to the least woman to toss her human life out and beyond suffering, privation, injustice, death, beyond the rim of the universe into the bosom of God. These may seem strange truths to be found in buses and subways, in kitchens and drawing-rooms; but they are not so strange. *The Catholic woman is never going merely from room to room in a house, from end to end of a city, from country to country; She is moving toward a goal outside the universe.* Her eyes do not stop at the crowded streets, at narrow walls, at the sky, the sea, and the earth. From the height of faith she sees the universe through the eyes of God; from that faulty miniature of the beauty of God, through those same divine eyes, she looks into the depths of infinite beauty, darkly, but drawn on, whatever the difficulty of the struggle, by the promise that dark glimpse holds out to her.

Faith can be hated for the hard things it demands, and the acid of distortion may be thrown in its face in a vain attempt to destroy the power of its beauty; it can be the victim of mockery by men in love with their blindness. It can be denied, rejected, lightly tossed aside. But then again, it can be lived up to, cherished, jealously guarded, proudly defended at whatever cost. In the latter case, the world looks on, blind to the beauty of actions that are robed in the splendor that comes from an object so high that properly it belongs to God: the vision of the face of God.

CHAPTER FOUR

Perfect Hostess

A N INVESTIGATOR who reports that a woman is a housewife, a lawyer, a painter, or a singer has brought in some information. On the contrary, if his statement puts her down as a hostess, he has left her occupation clothed in mystery. She may be pictured in a jaunty overseas cap and a full uniform smiling her way through the rarefied air of the Rockies at two or three hundred miles an hour; or, just as legitimately, in practically no uniform at all tossing her smile at clouds of smoke in a night club where speed is an entirely metaphorical thing. She may be an official on a crack train, the winner of a beauty contest presiding over a World's Fair, a glorified office girl at an industrial exhibition; in fact, she may be almost anything and still lay claim to the title of hostess. The definitions are legion.

Unquestionably these modern hostesses get tired of airsick, frightened or bored travelers, of spoiled babies, helpless mothers, of endless questions and boorish manners. Most of all, they must get very tired of producing a constant smile and a bright good humor. It must be a relief to them, at the end of a long day, to kick the discarded smile into a corner, even though its wrinkles will have to be ironed out in the morning; their grouches seem almost legitimate luxuries. And this, perhaps, is the best clue to the striking degeneration of the word "hostess."

The change took place when it became necessary to sell hospitality because all the world had become strangers to one another, and the traveler could find his ease only in proportion to the weight of his purse. Perhaps in other times there was not such a strain on hospitality, whether because home was so good or traveling so difficult. At any rate the change is best expressed in the transformation of what was originally a joy into a matter of an eight-hour working day.

The inferiority of the commercial product might be overlooked if it were not that the original brand of hospitality endures as long as there are homes whose doors open to those on the roads of the world. As it is, we can see clearly what a makeshift has been forced upon us by the necessities of a modern world. For the art of being a hostess is really not an art at all; rather it is a mystery, an intangible quality that eludes wealth, poverty, long planning, education, training.

In the concrete the thing is evident. One woman, at the end of a long, well considered preparation, may survey her work, as she awaits the arrival of her guest, and find it good indeed. She knows all the gestures, has all the equipment that wealth and good servants can offer, perhaps she even spent full days in school listening to the theory of this business of entertaining. Yet her guest is chilled. Throughout his visit he breathes an air of serene, aloof perfection akin to the cold beauty of blue moonlight piercing the bitter clear air to be rejected sharply by the hard surface of the virgin snow. He never forgets that perfection; it is something to escape from, something that penetrates to his very bones.

Another woman can be taken unawares by a surprise guest in her bare castle of poverty. Yet there is a subtle magic in her welcome. The wand is waved and the mismated china, the faded linen, the meager fare disappear from consideration for the rest of the visit. A warm cloak is thrown about the guest against the chill of the world. Doors swing open to him, and he walks into the alluring maze of a human heart, entranced by ever new beauties that seem to have been put away in secret places awaiting his coming. He is at home. He has enjoyed a thing that is not to be bought, cajoled, or stolen, but only to be given; and it is indeed a priceless gift.

Hospitality is not, of course, something proper to the poor or to the rich. Nowhere can a guest feel more ill at ease than in the presence of poverty's pride put to shame. The true hostess is not a product of her material possessions; indeed she is not the product of anything so much as of herself and the grace of God.

And, in a very real sense, every true hostess is a failure in her own eyes, unless she has underestimated her guest. In the last analysis, what word can she say, what gesture can she make, what gifts can she bring, what luxuries or comforts can she offer that will carry the authentic message of joyous welcome her heart is stuttering to speak? We have to take our love on faith; and it is a poor welcome indeed that is not flavored by love.

The hostess who bids her guest farewell, decidedly well satisfied with her success in providing for him, has been posing for a portrait by herself rather than welcoming a guest. Her efforts might have been courtesy's cool tolerance, superiority's mild amusement, indifference's bored routine, or sympathy's passing compassion.

All in all, the Catholic woman should be the world's best hostess, not merely because of her familiarity with love that is no less than divine, but also because no other woman has such perpetual practice, no other woman can ever be so intimate with the failure inevitable in a true welcome. The Catholic woman, you see, is forever welcoming God into her world, into her home, into her heart. And she is forever impressed with the inadequacy of the entertainment she has offered her divine guest.

Pere Monsabre has expressed the need for this unceasing welcome of divinity as only he could: "(God) appears to me in all things. All creatures, sharing a ray of His beauty, reveal His infinite perfections to me. The miseries of my brethren recall to me the sorrows of His dear Son. In everything that is contrary to me I recognize and adore His justice; in everything that is favorable to me I recognize and kiss His caressing hand. I see Him everywhere, and He sees me. My thoughts, my desires, my actions begin and develop under his benevolent and merciful eye."

As a matter of fact the Catholic woman's role as hostess to divinity has a much more personal note than this. As a small child she began to receive Holy Communion with the full consciousness that this meant receiving the Son of Mary into the house of her soul. Her preparations were solemnly serious, her entertainment of the royal guest a gay, utterly unself-conscious affair. She was "playing house" on a grand scale, and the game—which was not a game—gave reason enough for Christ's preference for little children.

From the beginning she used poverty's makeshift in welcoming her guest; the years have not changed the procedure in the least. She no longer resorts to the childish strategem of telling the Son of God a "ghost story" for fear a long silence might bore Him; but her dissatisfaction with her preparations and thanksgivings year after year tells the wholesome story of a hostess who has never done as much as she wanted to do for her divine visitor. Yet somehow through all the years she is smilingly pleased with each visit, not so much because of what she has contributed to its success but rather because of the assurance which is the supreme reward of every hostess, the assurance that her guest has been pleased, has been at home.

CHAPTER FIVE

Pocket Homes

THE DRUMS of war are always the signal for the fluttering flight of the dove of peace. The automatic break-up of the homes of men is an immediate and profound statement of war's destruction of peace: children by the million evacuated to safer places than home, men on the march away from home, so mysteriously on the march that their wives and mothers know only that they are "somewhere in . . . ," casuality lists to dash the hopes of reunion and break the heart in the open market place. Perhaps the same truth is expressed more graphically by the thunder of a bomb as it scatters the ashes of the hearth and the stones of the foundation to the four winds in a cloud of dust.

War is an ignominious, criminal thing so far as it is an attack on homes; it has its nobility only so far as it is a defense of homes. War destroys peace because war destroys homes and that for which homes stand. For the home is the most concrete, tangible expression of peace. In their homes, the members of a family share a common goal to which they move, sanctioned, encouraged, helped by each other. That family concord is possible because other families share with this one a still larger common goal to which they move in unison, and because each member of the individual family has gained a degree of mastery over himself, enjoys an inner peace which comes from the unity of his own appetites in seeking their common goal that is the last, the supreme end of the individual.

A building that houses a human group of selfish brawlers is not a home; it is a battlefield. A community whose families are at one another's throats to destroy and absorb, is not a community of homes but of forts subject to constant attack. An individual whose soul is a barren territory made sterile by the ceaseless tramp of warring appetites or who is the chained slave of his animal nature has not, cannot have a home; he is a marauder with no goal beyond the immediate present, no thought that escapes the narrow boundaries of himself.

At first glance it seems a little ridiculous that to destroy such a quiet, peaceful thing as a home, governmental decrees, high-power bombs, roaring airplanes, and military machines should be necessary—as silly as using a machine gun to fight off mosquitoes. It seems even more incredible that all this concentrated destruction is never entirely successful: homes are never utterly destroyed. But this note of the ridiculous, the incredible, is heard only because we have not appreciated the solid walls, the deep foundations, the mighty power of a home. A home is a rugged thing because peace has a rugged, enduring strength far beyond that of war.

Peace is not a matter of a moment's thought or a day's effort. It is not a flimsy shack thrown up in a week. It takes long in building and is hard come by. Indeed it is a strong, hard thing. Into it must go a personal mastery whose accomplishment will tax the efforts of any man or woman until the day of death; only those who are kings of their own souls can hope for peace. Peace demands that authentic gesture of love which is sacrifice, and the long, calm view of distant goals that shrinks the petty obstacles of the moment into insignificance. Peace is accomplished, in other words, through justice, charity, and wisdom; the guns capable of destroying such as these can never be made. These are not carried by storm, they must be surrendered by treachery and cowardice.

Perhaps all this could be put into a tiny locket of words that fits easily next to our hearts: war destroys peace because it makes vagabonds of men, and men are not easily made vagabonds.

Yet here we are faced with the paradox of the Prince of Peace, who was a divine vagabond. Such is His own description of Himself: "The Son of man has not whereon to lay His head." Nor was this an exaggeration. The low hanging stars of Palestine's quiet nights formed the roof that most frequently sheltered His sleep. The apostles learned their lessons from Him, not within four walls, but walking in the porch of the Temple, sitting on the hillside, crowding the shore of the lake, walking the dusty roads or huddled in a small boat tossing on the sea. He would say good-bye under a human roof that His friends might savor the last echo of His words; but for Himself, He would endure His agony in the rock-strewn Garden of Olives and give up His last breath under the open sky.

Indeed He made a vagabond of His mother. Hardly had He taken flesh when she traveled the length of the land to visit her cousin. He was born practically on the high road, in a cave near a strange city. He was lost in Jerusalem for three days. Vagabondage seems to have been a condition for discipleship under the Master, for His disciples were to leave father, mother, brother, and sister, and to follow Him; indeed they were even to deny themselves. The bold Peter, the fiery Paul, the loving John, the silent Matthew, the tardy Thomas, they and their fellows tested foot by foot the long roads of Rome and went beyond them, vagabond conquerors of the world for Christ.

Yet for all that there was no place where they were not at home, just as there was no place occupied by Christ and His mother that was not home. Where our Lord was, where His mother was, there was to be found justice, love, and its sacrifice, the far, wise view of the last goal: the things that home stands for and by which home stands. The vagabond Prince of Peace looms as the home maker of the world without whom there are only invasion, selfishness, mad scrambling for the glittering tinsel of the moment, and no hope of home.

He is a lover of vagabonds to insist that His followers cut the ties that bind a man. Perhaps this insistence is to remind us that, like Himself, we, too, are always at war though never losing peace, that we, too, while never homeless are always without a home, travelers on the wide road of life that leads at last to home. It is not easy to be on guard against an enemy whose alertness never slackens; it is not a simple thing to avoid mistaking the cozy shelter by the roadside for a permanent protection against the wind, the rain, the heat, the cold, the weight of the sky, and the ominous uncoiling of the road. Only such a flashing paradox as a warrior Prince of Peace, a homeless vagabond always at home, could light up even the darkest, most dangerous stretches of the road.

Men, however, are not easily made vagabonds, even in the name of splendid, divine things. Joyce Kilmer adhered closely to facts when he wrote in *Roofs*:

"I never have seen a vagabond who really liked to roam
All up and down the streets of the world and not to have a home:
He'll sit on the grass and take his ease so long as the sun is high,
But when it is dark he wants a roof to keep away the sky.
And the only reason a road is good, as every wanderer knows,
Is just because of the homes, the homes, the homes to which it goes."

It is but a repetition of that poignant plaint of the Lord Himself: "The Son of man has not whereon to lay his head." St. Dominic knew well that thirst for home as he sat there alone in the quiet of evening outside the walls of Fanjeaux, the lowering Pyrenees at his back and stretched out at his feet the rich plains of southern France, the farms crowding one another good-naturedly, the towns scattered by a prodigal hand. But even to one well acquainted with the thoughtfulness of divine love, it must have been startling to receive that unexpected, spontaneous caress from the Mother of God, which has since come to be known as the Rosary. Who but the Mother of God could have conceived of a home that men could carry in their pockets?

A collapsible home, unfolded in an instant in the deserts where men roam! The child evacuated from the city, the soldier at the end of the day's march, the wife gazing numbly at the ruins of her house, each lets the beads slip through his fingers; the centuries slip away, and they are back again with Mary and her Son.

It is not strange that the rosary is worn at the left side of every Dominican, like an unsheathed sword; or that Rosary Sunday should commemorate the clash and roar of one of the great battles of history. The Rosary is a prayer of war time, a prayer for homeless men. At the same time it is pre-eminently a prayer of peace. It is a prayer to be said by the family gathered in the sanctuary of the home.

> "For men are homesick in their homes,
> And strangers under the sun,
> And they lay their heads in a foreign land
> Whenever the day is done."

It is the prayer that brings us to Mary and her Son; where they are is home, however loud the thunder of guns, the roar of a mob, the appalling shamble of ruined cities, the torn bodies of men. There is peace that is not to be uprooted by any instrument devised by the ingenuity of men. They, Mary and her Son, are the house to which the feet of men and women make their weary way.

> "Here we have battle and blazing eyes,
> And chance and honour and high surprise,
> But our homes are under miraculous skies
> Where the yule tale was begun.
> To an open house in the evening
> Home shall men come,
> To an older place than Eden
> And a taller town than Rome.
> To the end of the way of the wandering star,
> To the things that cannot be and that are,
> To the place where God was homeless
> And all men are at home."

CHAPTER SIX

Dream of a Child

THE BEAUTY of our actions is most vivid where there is least or most of it. To our always childish eyes the steady flame of a quiet fire goes unnoticed beside the brilliance of a spark burning its life out in a splendid instant, or the roaring flame of a raging conflagration. For an instant a sinner, enslaved by things of sense, escapes from the sluggish depths to produce an act that transcends the material, a product of reason and free will. It is only a spark, but it fires our memory of the innate dignity and power for good and evil in us all. The hero's spurning of the cautious values of petty men is a roaring flame to which we do not approach too closely, but from which we cannot tear our eyes. The saint's actions are a searing pencil of white heat, delicate in its fineness, terrible in its intensity, needing no protection from the threat of wind, rain, or storm. From the least to the greatest, the beauty and power of our actions are accurately judged by the predominance of the spiritual, the superiority over the material.

Philosophically this is, no doubt, the explanation of the fact that a child always holds the center of the stage of the world, that a child's feast must always hold the hearts and minds of men; though it is not a justification of the adults' appropriation of the children's toys. For the child is, in a very real sense, an incarnation of the supreme beauty of man's natural actions. Certainly now the high point of human activity is found in love. Here man shakes off not only the cumbersome chains of external things, the clinging, enfeebling embrace of the senses; he shakes off his very self. That identification of wills, involved in love's essential notion of wishing good to another, means that a human individual has exceeded himself, has found another self, achieved a new life, new interests, new activities. Yet all of these, while they are his own, are still not his but another's.

Love's activities are an attempt to give expression to this deep union, to deny self and assert identity with the loved one. However, the language it uses fails as ludicrously as the infant's gurgles. Handshakes, kisses, embraces, the intimacies of married life, even the strong words of sacrifice still leave the central fact of love something not definitely expressed, not clear to the eyes of the mind, still to be taken on faith. The child is an embodiment of all that love has tried to say. He is the child, not of one parent, but of both; his characteristics, his features, everything about him is a blend of the lovers who generated him. Yet he is neither one nor the other. In a sense he is both; yet he is a distinct, responsible, sacred individual.

Understandably, then, Christmas is an emotional rallying point. Here the hearts of men, women, and children are stirred by the dramatic presentation of a profound yearning of the human heart, the sacred circle of father, mother, and infant; here all hearts are torn by the exposure of that universal group to neglect and discomfort. It is the meeting place of the "things that cannot be and that are," for here are the spotless virgin and the helpless Infant, who is almighty God.

Precisely because Christmas is the birthday of a *divine* infant it is much more than all this. It is a compact summary of the superior beauty of divine love, as well as of the highest of human hopes and human activities; it is the realization of a dream, higher, more beautiful than love's dream, a dream for which men have yearned or from which they have fled since the dawn of the human race. Christmas tells the story, in one picture, of a ceaseless striving after, or a desperate attempt to escape from, a God who can never be escaped and never fully attained in the world of men; the shepherds, the Magi, and Herod, are a necessary part of that picture.

This striving by man for the divine, this attempt to reach not only out of himself, but out of the world in which he lives, ranges from the foredoomed attempt of mystic eastern religions to storm the walls of the supernatural with armaments forged by nature, to the snickering deification of dissolute Roman emperors. The flight of men from their God runs the gamut from the cowardice of Greek metaphysics, down the ages, to the resoundingly empty atheist of today, who would destroy God by shouting Him down, by making Him a robot of science, or by applying to Him the twentieth-century epithet: Thou art He who never is, Thou art ceaseless becoming.

But God is not to be escaped. "In Him we live and move, and have our being." Our very existence is a sip out of the cup of divine being, a participation in that activity that never began. It is something which does not belong to human nature in its own right, that cannot be found in any analysis of the ingredients of human nature; but which, nevertheless, can be found in everything that is. All things borrow a bit of life from the Creditor who has the fullness of life.

In the world of thought we seek the truth that will make us free. A great truth is discovered: men see the silhouette of a divine perfection. We are enraptured by beauty and, behold, it is only God's shadow on earth. We are caught in the whirl of a busy world only to see its clumsy slowness imaging dimly the Pure Act who is always. We cling desperately to youth only to have it change to old age in our hands, leaving us face to face with the changeless God of ages. Sin becomes our guide only to lead us to the most just Judge. Love inspires us only to teach us what things we must suffer in His name who is love.

The coming of Christ is the climax wherein the inescapable and unattainable God becomes man. It is the focal point of human thought and action; *anno Domini,* the year of the Lord who is man. This is the end and the beginning; the point of union between God and man that must forever draw the eyes of all sons of Adam to its cave in the hills of Judea.

Reason, especially in a cynical age such as ours, will protest that God remains God, and man, man. The two cannot be thrown together like ingredients of a chemical mixture.

But here at Christmas we are invited to look at that mysterious union in which man is complete, body, soul, mind, will, flesh, blood, and bones; and God is still that unutterable array of unified perfection that is divinity. Neither one is destroyed, neither is sacrificed; yet these two are one. And it is unequivocally true that this man is God, and God is this man, Jesus Christ.

The divinely conceived bond of union is that mysterious thing we call personality, what the philosophers call subsistence. We can grasp something of this perfection of subsistence from a consideration of the Christmas story itself. Even admitting the crowded condition of Bethlehem that night, the spectacle of a young pregnant mother turned away from shelter in midwinter might well evoke the comment: What an inhuman thing to do! By such a statement we are avowedly not thinking of the persons responsible, rather, in defense of our own nature, we are condemning this act as not the kind that proceeds from a human *nature.* If our indignation goes further and we ask, who did this, then we are seeking not *nature,* but the *person* who is responsible. Personality, subsistence, is this last note which comes to the individual nature and makes it stand up of itself, subsist, be responsible.

This is another of those perfections we borrow in a poor, limited fashion from God, as we borrow our existence. It is something not to be found in the analysis of the essential elements of humanity; rather it is to be grasped only when the limitations of humanity and the unlimited nature of divinity are compared. In the poor vessel of our humanity we can receive only so much of this perfection of subsistence, and call it human subsistence, human personality; the angels, for all their preeminence, bring only a greater pitcher to the divine well to receive angelic subsistence. But it is only in God Himself that subsistence without limit is to be found.

On that first Christmas night the angels announced to the world what had been told to the Virgin long months ago in Nazareth: that the nature of man, full and complete, had been brought to the side of the completely perfect divine nature, and the infinite personality of the divine Being had taken the place of the faint image that would have been human personality. The original stood in the place of its representation, and the nature of God and the nature of man were upheld by one and the same infinite personality of the Son of God. Thus was the seemingly impossible accomplished, the eternal quest terminated, the hopes of humanity realized, God made man.

From that first night in Bethlehem, every breath drawn by that Infant was an act of God, every toddling step as He grew older, was a step of God. Every word He spoke in Palestine was a word of God; every instant of suffering in His passion was the suffering of God. All possessed of the infinite value attached to the works of divinity. These were human things, acts that proceeded from a human nature. Who did these things? God, the Second Person of the Blessed Trinity. This helpless Infant is Savior, Redeemer, Lord, God, a divine person; but also the son of the Maid of Galilee.

The story is old. Before Bethlehem it was a dream; after that holy night, a memory that never dies. It is an old, old story which ties the first man to the last with the unbreakable bonds of love's wonders, hopes, and high goals. The Christmas picture is one of peace: Joseph, Mary, and the Infant. Its message is always the same: peace to men, whatever the condition of the world in any age. It is a childlike, serene peace; peace in the knowledge that the hearts of men and God are not to be changed, that the dream goes on, and its realization is an eternal thing.

CHAPTER SEVEN

On Growing Younger

CONSIDERED SUPERFICIALLY, it might seem a strange thing that we insist on celebrating Christmas at home. At Christmas, all arteries of travel are choked with homeward-bound men and women, on their way to celebrate the homelessness of Christ. It still remains true that where Mary and her Son were homeless, there are all men at home. Indeed, wherever Mary and her Son are, there is home for the Catholic heart, whether it be the high road, a cave on the hillside, or the bare crown of a hill just outside the walls of Jerusalem.

With the holiday season over and the advent of a new year, the sons and daughters, of all ages, rewrite a portion of their lives by starting out again from home and into the world. It is as though the years had dropped away in a moment of phantasy, taking with them the portliness of the matron, the bare spaces of the executive's thinning hair, the worn face etched by worry and suffering. Our hearts are young again, our carriage a little gangling, our eyes on fire, the road before us very long and very bright.

The old year is dead, and the infant year invites us to stop a moment and play with it. The momentary contact renews our hope, polishes up the bright goals of youth, lengthens the future, revitalizes our energy, and sets us to planning again the many hard things the years have somehow left undone. The page of the old year, with all its blots, mistakes, failures, and sorrows is turned over; in its place is the virgin page of the new year, its unsullied beauty capturing our hearts and minds so completely as to wipe from our memory the unpleasantness of the past. We are young again, with practically no past and a long, long future. We are starting over again, and life takes on the zest of adventure, the novelty of the unknown.

We might think it a pleasant coincidence that New Year's Day falls on the feast of the christening of the Son of Mary, if we did not know that there are no coincidences in the divine plans. It is not by coincidence that a river flows just here, a mountain stands there, a star burns its path to this particular eye. These things were set out by the hand of God with a greater care and deliberation than a housewife devotes to setting out the silver and china for a very special dinner; nor did the divine hand get tired, shaky, or bored with setting the table of the universe. It is not by chance but with profound significance that we of the twentieth century celebrate the beginning of the year and the conferring of the name of Jesus on the Son of Mary, for not even the man-made computations of time escape divine providence.

In a sense we might say that God thus turned a childish fantasy of ours into a reality. It is as though God had listened in on our bedtime stories, taken His omnipotent action, and then stood back to watch our wide-eyed astonishment as we saw the characters walk out of our dreams to join us in our midnight snack. For, of course, without Christ the renewed youth, vanished past, resurrected future, and all the things we associate with the beginning of a new year are no more than a pleasant fiction. To tear a page off a calendar is not at all the same thing as to tear a year out of a man's life; we can blur the record with the eraser of forgetfulness, but we cannot obliterate the characters we have pressed so deeply into the days of a year. A man cannot re-enter his mother's womb and be born again, it is not given to man to rewrite any portion of his life, youth is not recaptured and home ties broken afresh simply because it is January. The new year is not a new-born child, but one more wrinkle—drawn by Time's relentless fingers on the worn face of the universe.

In other words, a few weeks after the new year has started on its way, the fiction is worn thin even to our wishful minds.

We know beyond question that we have gotten no younger; that the past is still there with its accusations and plentiful evidence; that a totally new start is impossible with this burden of the years strapped firmly to our backs.

It would be too much to expect of any numbered revolutions of the planets to give us back youth, wipe out the past, and furnish us with a new start; but not at all too much to expect from God's kindly consideration of human weakness. The coming of the Son of Mary was a crystallization of this dream among many others. It was beautifully fitting that we should see Him thus, so pitifully small and helpless, only eight days old at the close of His brief period of anonymity when His only identification could be by reference to His mother: the Son of Mary whose name had not yet been whispered except by the angel. He was so very young, with only the past of eternity to prepare Him for the moment of time, making the start that would renew the face of the earth and the courts of heaven.

We might say that in that private christening which conferred the name of Jesus on the Son of God there was a pantomime of the actualization of the long dreams of men. In Him our youth is renewed, not once or twice, not once a year, but always and eternally. In fact the more we grow up as children of God, the younger we get: we reverse the natural process, growing closer and closer to our divine Parent, realizing more and more profoundly our utter dependence on Him, approaching more and more rapidly that boundary between time and eternity whose crossing will confer an eternal youth. All our lives we are more dependent on Him than ever we were on mother or father; all through life our sins will maintain the awful, tragic terror of that first childish sin that sent us then, as sin does now, rushing in an agony of remorse to the One who welcomes children and keeps them young. In a sense, it is only by sin that we grow irrevocably old.

From this point of view, we have already been given eternity's mastery over time. A moment on our knees, and the horrors of the mistakes of the past disappear from the history of the world as though we had reached behind us into the days and years, plucked them out of their place, and exposed them to the brightness of divine sunlight for the instant necessary to annihilate them. We are master architects sharing something of the power of the Creator's omnipotent *fiat*. We come to the end of blind alleys of sin and are hemmed in like a beast in a dark cage, with no outlet for our minds, our hearts, our feet. A whispered word to the Infant who was christened Savior, and before us stretches the highway, sweeping magnificently over the hills and valleys, on into the infinite distances like a full-blooded steed scorning the earth. Again we have the long goals, the high hopes, the great tasks that keep the eyes young peering into the distance, the heart racing in the great adventure, the arm strong to strike the lusty blows that must be struck to complete the long trek home.

Or, to put it in another way, that infant Son of Mary on His christening day, was a personification of the virtue of youth, the virtue that has the short, brisk name of hope. He is the goal which hope's eyes discern even though they must peer through the grime of a tenement, the smoke of a factory, or the tiny windows of a cottage. In Him are the omnipotence, the mercy, the fidelity which course through the veins of hope, warding off the collapse of despair's weakness and the paralysis of presumption's high blood pressure. He is the eternally young Son of the Father, as He was then the very young Son of Mary, the Word by whom everything was made. Hope is young, gloriously young. It does not look to God as a source of truth as does faith, nor as a goal as does charity, but as a beginning, a beginning of successful action. Of course it has a spring to its step, a lilt to its heart, a light in its eyes, and a smile of confidence that is solidly justified.

But, like all youth, hope is a realistic thing. It can know fear and caution; for it knows the fight that must be made before the goal is attained. It is not at all to be confused with that caricature of hope that goes by the name of sentiment and is age's substitute for youth. Really, we have done youth an injustice by picturing it as a time of dreams; it does not so much dream as plan. Age does the dreaming, drifting blindly on waves of memory and emotion, mistaking a wishful feeling of security for victory finally achieved. And this is particularly clear in a world that has grown old, irrevocably old by a gaping separation from its Father. It will drown the past in a drunken stupor and wake up hugging to its breast the fiction of a new start, an obliterated past, and a restored youth. But not for long; indeed, only for as long as it takes to meet a new difficulty, another failure, a ghost from the past, any of which will be mirror enough to make plain the battered, weary, lonely status of a soul that was made to stay young. Only through God was there a first beginning; and only through His Son are other beginnings granted to men. The Son of Mary is the eternally young Son of the Father; only in His name can men hold fast to youth.

CHAPTER EIGHT

Of Age and Innocence

THERE MAY be a smiling glimmer of eternity in the fact that the very old never quite escape youth, and the very young are so much at home in the world that is far from youthful. For in eternity, the eternally young and the eternally old are united, not only in the cohorts of the blessed, but in the vision of God. It takes some neat side-stepping of the evidence to see youth and old age staring at each other across an impassable chasm; we have to dodge the hurtling power of a significant truth to see them glaring as from enemy camps.

The fact is that old age and youth have an affinity for each other as irresistible as the immediate companionship of a boy and a dog. They belong together. The ancients were the men who roamed the earth when the world was young. The Fathers of the Church are the giants whose voices roared their message over the blare of Roman trumpets when the Church was only a few hundred years old. But the truth is deeper than our association of hoary venerability with the beginning of things. It gives meaning to facts that fairly dance in their attempts to attract our attention.

Old age is too often a lonely stretch of idle years, because it lacks its natural complement of grandchildren; the simmering energy and supple activity of children is a restless, uneasy thing deprived of the easy camaraderie, the stability, the quiet of one the fires of whose energy can be rekindled only by an eternal torch and whose bones will cease to ache only at the magic whisper of death.

The very old and the very young belong together. The old, by a long, slow, painful progress, have climbed to the heights of old age. There they stand, with life stretched out behind and beneath them, seeing clearly now what the dust and fog and smoke of the things that go into life hid from their eyes so long. They have a mellow clarity of vision to be matched only by the penetrating innocence of one who has hardly started life, to whom games are only games, to whom characters are revealed by a gesture, and to whom truth is obviously to be faced, not escaped.

Both of them, the young and the old, share the same long, long horizons: the first, fresh from the hand of God, still looks out over the edge of the world; the second, ready for God, looks back steadily from the edge of the world and forward into the vastness of eternity. Both have a realistic sense of values that puts all others to shame. Neither is fooled by pretense in spite of silent submission to the efforts of the boaster, the four-flusher, the snob. Nothing is so wearing on the gaudy garments of hypocrisy as contact with the unyielding, unsmiling eyes of the old and the young. Both are proudly loyal to very few and very great objects of devotion, for to both mystery is an easy, natural thing; and love is essentially mysterious.

There is sound reason for our great pity for a world that is only modern, a world that bows only to youth; for this must be a world that is restless, uneasy, a stranger to the quiet, the stability, the companionship of the ages that huddle about the fire warming their old bones. There is a deep human basis for our horror of the fate of parents who will be old alone.

There is, then, a humanly satisfying light in the picture of the child Mary and her divine Son Whose Father was as old as eternity. Mary was close to God, the youth of her innocence to the timelessness of His enduring; they could be companions in the mysteriously satisfying way of a very tiny child and a very old man. Between Mary and God there would be, vaguely, a similarity of clear vision: the one the clarity of sinlessness, of unhampered reason and unlimited grace; the other of divine perfection; from her heights of sanctity she could see something of the vista that opened beneath the heights of His divinity; to her eyes, as she walked arm in arm with the God of things as they are, the real values would stand forth bravely making their inviolable claim to her heart, while the false slunk away from the clear light of her beauty.

To Mary there would be nothing of the questioning or bewilderment that confuses our minds in reading the story of her purification. With her young eyes fixed on the old eyes of God, she could see the crystalline truth and entrancing justice of His demand: "Sanctify unto me every first-born, for they are mine." There would be no hesitation in her compliance with the law's demand for a double sacrifice, one for holocaust and one for sin; even though she had nothing that was not already consumed with the fire of charity,—the very child she carried in her arms was Himself God—nothing that could even remotely resemble the disfigurement of sin. Because they were such comrades, this youthful virgin and the eternal God, she would smile in gratitude at another evidence of His gentle thoughtfulness of the poor, insisting that they be not excluded from divine things, rather than blush at a public statement of her poverty in the law's concession: "if her hand find not sufficiency, and she is not able to offer a lamb, she shall take two turtle doves or two young pigeons, one for a holocaust and one for sin: and the priest shall pray for her, and so she shall be cleansed."

I often wonder about the only priest who prayed for Mary instead of to her. Did he not feel a little supercilious about it at the time, even though he could not know what a miracle of grace she was? What a life he must have led afterward with the grateful arms of Mary's prayers encircling him, protecting him, strengthening him! What a treat it would have been to see the astonishment on his face his first day in heaven, when he found his clumsy prayers had been for the Queen of heaven and the Mother of priests! For all that he must, even yet, be supremely grateful at the fruits of that routine prayer in the simple ceremony of purification; for just as her Son, once helped by a man to carry His cross, thereafter helped all men to carry theirs, so Mary, once prayed for by a priest, has not ceased to pray for all priests.

The feast of the purification, however, is a heart-satisfying thing even in the purely human order from its contact of youth with age. Mary, remember, was very young, perhaps fifteen or sixteen. To see her carrying her infant Son to the Temple for this ceremony is to see the contrast between the Temple's marble vastness, its richness, its impressive grandeur, and the poverty, the obscurity, the childishness of Mary lost in its hugeness. Then, before she could get to the priest to offer her Son, her Child was taken from her childish arms by a stranger, an old man named Simeon.

Because he was very old and very holy, working intensely at still greater sanctity, there would be instant understanding, companionship between himself and the child-mother. Mary's bewilderment would hardly have time to turn into fright, for innocent youth and holy old age do understand each other. Mary's eyes darting in a hurried search to the face of Simeon would tell her in one glance all she needed to know in this first trusting of her Son to the hands of men.

Of course this understanding of youth and age is not limited to one sex; that there be no mistake about this, a very old and very holy old woman, Anna, played her part in the instant recognition of the Child and His welcome to the world of men. There is an interesting difference in the roles of the two, Simeon and Anna. To Anna was given that peculiarly satisfying task of telling the story, not in a gossipy, indiscriminate fashion, but yet not stingily to a few; rather to all who looked for the coming of the Savior. To Simeon was allotted the humbling, inspiring, breathtaking glance deep into the heart of the Mother of God; he it was who first saw that heart torn open that all other hearts might feel free to swing wide their gates to one whose heart was so like their own. Eternity is mirrored in the purification of Our Lady; then her heart will indeed be opened with the easy grace of one at home, a home where young and old are united in a ceaselss activity and quiet stability, unaging youth and timeless eternity.

CHAPTER NINE

Patient Answers

THE DEAD quiet of night echoed the footsteps of Nicodemus as he skulked to the feet of Christ, fearful of discovery but driven on by a question that had to be answered: "Can a man enter a second time his mother's womb, and be born again?" The glory of the dawn was outshone by the splendor of the risen Christ when the first Easter shouted to the ends of the earth that death had died. These two items from the crowded life of the Son of God seem as far apart as day and night; yet they belong together. The question had to be answered; and the full answer came only in the glory of the resurrection.

Nicodemus belongs in the Easter parade, even though he covered himself with the darkness of night and avoided the eyes of all men. The glory of Easter is missed if we emphasize only the aspect of birth in nature's glowing face and delicately fragrant garments, forgetting the dark womb of winter from which that birth proceeded. We have only part of the joy of our own gay raiment if we have lost sight of what is beneath and behind it. Birth, you know, is not something that happens in a joyously unsuspected instant; it is long and mysteriously secret in its preparation. To think otherwise is to be guilty of an absurdity not unlike the modern fable of a world that came from itself before it was.

In other words, the splendor of Easter morning has little meaning without the darkness of the night that preceded it; there can be no Easter without darkness of the tomb from which the glorious Christ stepped. Man must be born again, born from the womb of death, to life; it is not birth to life, but birth to life through death, Christ's and our own, that tells the full story of Easter. No one in our day has said this more perfectly than Francis Thompson:

"For there is nothing lives but something dies,
And there is nothing dies but something lives.
Till skies be fugitives,
Till time, the hidden root of change, updries,
Are Birth and Death inseparable on earth;
For they are twain yet one, and Death is Birth."

Perhaps this is why we have the real Easter so entirely to ourselves; for to us, the truth of death is simple—and lovely. Indeed this is why we have human life to ourselves. For it is only by facing death that we can taste of life, above all of life's supreme and fullest last moment. Shrinking from the very thought of death the better to embrace life is to have life slip from our arms and to meet death face to face even though we live.

The inestimable significance of the resurrection of our Lord makes us careless of wondrous details that are like a child's dreams suddenly come true: the mysteriously yawning tomb, the shining angels sitting so comfortably as they wait to astonish the women, the glorified body of the risen Master now here, now there, like flashing lightning splitting the darkness of pagan hopelessness. And the strangely contagious stupefaction of the guards that so affected the princes of the keenest merchant race on earth that they paid out good hard money for men to say they were asleep and to give testimony to what they saw in their dreams. Dreams C. O. D.!

Perhaps the most wondrous detail of all, though certainly the most unobtrusive and the most persistently neglected, is the softly persistent divine patience that lights up the whole story of the resurrection. Humanly speaking, God might very well have washed His hands of men after the resurrection was an accomplished fact. He had come among them taking the form of a slave, the helplessness of an infant. He had lived intimately with them. Hour after hour, day after day, He had turned the light of His divine wisdom and the power of His divinity on their dull minds, teaching them the secrets of more abundant life. He had loved them, suffered for them, died in disgrace for them; and as a last confirmation of their wavering faith, had risen from the dead. Now let them believe and have life, or let them doubt and throw life away!

But that is all humanly speaking. From the divine viewpoint, the apostle and disciples were to do all our doubting for us; and because it would always be easier for men to believe the sleeping witnesses, each doubt was patiently met and devastatingly demolished. He had come that we might have life and have it more abundantly; and this central fact of His resurrection was essential to that possession of life.

To quiet the feeble doubts of the wholesome, simple ones, a little testimony would be enough: such as the word of the angels which swept clear the hearts of the women of their doubts and fears; or the words of the Scriptures which set afire the hearts of the two saddened disciples on their way to Emmaus, though there, by way of divine largess, their eyes would be opened and a miracle tossed in as a parting gift.

But not all men are so wholesomely simple; the proud would doubt every detail, so every detail must be patiently manifested. Would they doubt the reality of His body? Let them "handle and see, for a spirit hath not flesh and bones as you see Me to have." One does not take a phantom by the arm or give an hallucination a piece of fish. Would they doubt the humanity of that body or its identity with the one that hung on the cross? Well these simple, straightforward fishermen knew men; this was no stranger from another world masquerading as a man. And after three years' eating, sleeping, walking with Him, they knew Christ; no one of them could forget the dead body they had reverently put in the tomb. "He showed them His hands and His side. The disciples therefore were glad when they saw the Lord. . . . Then He saith to Thomas: Put in thy finger hither, and see My hands; and bring hither thy hand, and put it into My side; and be not faithless, but believing."

A soulless zombie, perhaps? Oh no. As well doubt the presence of our own souls. After all, a soul is not a gown to be hung in a closet or fingered lovingly to convince ourselves of its reality; it is to be recognized by its powers breaking into act: nutritive, sensitive and intellectual powers. "But while they yet believed not, and wondered for joy, He said: Have you here anything to eat? . . . And when He had eaten before them, taking the remains, He gave to them." On the sensitive side, well at least He had eyes, ears, and a tongue, and He used them; for He recognized the disciples, spoke to them, answered their questions. He discoursed on the Scriptures, gave last-minute instructions, comforted the brethren, all of which demanded intellect.

All that argued for the humanity of the risen Savior. Of course someone, at some time, would doubt His divinity. Very well, let them explain that last little drama on the shores of the Sea of Galilee. "And that night they caught nothing. But when the morning was come, Jesus stood on the shore: yet the disciples knew not that it was Jesus. Jesus therefore said to them: Children, have you any meat? They answered Him: No. He saith to them: Cast the net on the right side of the ship and you shall find. They cast therefore; and now they were not able to draw it, for the multitude of fishes. That disciple therefore whom Jesus loved, said to Peter: It is the Lord." Or let them stand on the hill looking over the walls into the city of Jerusalem, or stopping their glance halfway up the slope at the Garden still wet with His blood, and explain how He ascended into heaven before a crowd of witnesses.

This was Jesus Christ, true God and true man, body and blood, soul and divinity; but newly risen from the dead. He, too, had put on fresh garments, the garments of immortality. This was no longer the stumbling, beaten victim of a blood-mad mob. He entered into their midst through closed doors, He vanished before their eyes, He came to places miles apart in the flick of an eyelash. For in heaven, they shall be like angels.

God was very patient with the doubters; and still is. Yet we can even understand something of this divine patience, wonder less at it, when we remember the results of it. For the fact that patience insisted on, the fundamental fact of the resur-

rection of the crucified Son of Mary, was the confirmation of
the faith that released man from the prison of the universe. From
it was struck the undying hope that sparks the courage of the
only men in the world who do not know how to surrender. It
gives the confident answer to all the long dreams of love's unquenchable thirsts. It was, indeed, worth being patient about.
For Christ came that we might have life. And man lives to learn
to die; he dies that he may live undyingly. The tomb is open
on Easter morning; but there must be a tomb as a gateway to
glory.

CHAPTER TEN

Effective Loving

THE WORST of hack writers now and then faces the impossibility of squeezing a thought into a word that is too small for it. The word may wear with some degree of comfort for a short time, but the comfort is an illusion that is not long in being shattered. The word, from the first instant, is cramping, distorting the thought until finally, in desperation, the thought shrieks in protest or gives up the struggle and resigns itself to distortion.

This should not be true with all the thousands of words the English language has begged, borrowed, or stolen. There are so many; surely fingering through them we can find what we want. Yet, as a matter of fact, it sometimes seems as though these words were literary gold that had ceased to be recognized as legal tender, leaving their possessors starving for expression.

Take, for example, the words we can muster in an attempt to express the mysteriously effective activity of love. We can speak of "kindliness" and call up pictures of gentle old ladies in lavender and lace, but helpless old ladies; or, of "benevolence" and seeing ourselves surrounded by well-wishers, back-patters who are quite willing to have us call on them for anything we need sometime, but not now. There is "beneficence," but that is the beggar's correlative that stamps the gullible victim of a cadger; "philanthropy" operates only on a big scale, with fitting publicity and a certain degree of pompousness; just plain "help" may mean anything from holding the baby to routing burglars.

At least none of these, in ordinary usage, has a necessary, let alone an intimate, connection with love.

Yet there should be a word to say what love tries so desperately to say in action. Love means to wish good to another and the will is effective of its desires (when it does not confuse desire with mere vague wishing); the divine, universally efficacious will is particularly and infallibly effective. When we talk of the driving effectiveness of divine love we have something that is really worth saying. But it cannot be said in any one word; nor in any series of words. Indeed, its whole story will never be known by anyone but God, though we shall have a decidedly good digest of it in heaven. To help us through the discouragement of our stumbling words, the Lord Himself wrote a metaphor in nature which men have come to call the month of April.

For a few minutes reflection makes it clear that the divine love hovers over the life of man with the vivacious persistence of April calling earth to life.

At least it is not hard to see that human life is a stolid earth, chilled from its first turning aside from the divine Sun; it is sluggish, somber, slow to respond, bare. Mediocrity's wide kingdom is a barren plain that stretches to horizons wider than we dare imagine; old age's too often empty hands lifted against the sky present a starker, more tragic picture than the barren limbs of the oldest, most worn-out tree. The reluctance with which we surrender our pet slavery, the eagerness with which we toss away the staunch freedom of our souls are protests against life more vocal, deeper, more frightening than the bad-tempered grumblings of earth on being awakened from its winter sleep. The call to heights of that heroic human activity which is sanctity is not answered by mobs but by a handful of eager, reckless, gallant youngsters whatever be their age; just as it is only the young, eager, reckless things of earth that push to answer spring's call to come out and live.

Surely divine love has April's unpredictable moods. Sometimes it is gay with the naively complete gaiety of a child's communion; again, with exuberant gaiety of release that rushes

into the soul just emptied of sin; or the ecstatic, utterly generous
gaiety of consecration that ties together so closely the bride's
veil, the nun's vow, and the oil on the priest's hands. Such gay
love it was that made Paul's world-wide journeys erratic, breath-
taking flights rather than grim marches; that sat the vivacious
Magdalene so contentedly at the feet of Christ, that made Peter
and John's account of the Sanhedrin's questioning sound so much
like a child's boasting tale.

Sometimes that divine love is as serenely smiling as a guile-
less April sky. There was, you remember, the peace of those
quiet walks along the roads of Palestine while Christ listened
to the small talk of His disciples; the inestimably precious
evenings by the Lake of Genesareth when the lessons of the day
were gone over so patiently and the wise calm of the divine voice
seemed a part of the evening's rest. There were the bright cloudless mornings when the sorrows of yesterday seemed wiped from
the pages of history; the easy familiar discussions in that beloved
house at Bethany.

Yet there were, too, the moments of frightening thunder.
There was the terrifying echo of "Thou shalt not" in His
solemn words; there was little room for compromising comfort
in the finality of His judgment of worthy followers as those
who, hand to the plow, do not look back. It was not a
soothing demand He made when He said: "If you love Me,
keep My commandments"; rather it was a challenge to battle,
to ceaseless battle. He was not speaking in metaphors when
He spoke of the everlasting fire that awaited those who were
conquered by the life they were afraid to live.

Nor was all this mere noise to terrorize men into living.
These were the sharp, quick, unexpected devastating strokes of
lightning that seared the souls of men. His contemptuous,
explosive "hypocrites"; His sharp dismissal of Peter: "Get
thee behind Me, Satan"; the shamed repentance of the sinner
that His very eyes demanded as they sought the waste of
the soul for a resting place of peace.

Beneath all that gaiety, serenity, thunder and lightning,
there ran a current of strength: a strength that awoke men's

hearts to unsuspected heights of fertility, that brought forth patient understanding from the violent Peter, ceaseless preaching and writing from the silent Matthew, prompt response to martyrdom from the tardy Thomas. It was a strength that blossomed in the inexhaustible activity of all who came into contact with it, not merely in the one outstanding example of Paul; it unveiled unsuspected beauties that outshone the things April finds in the depths of earth's powers; it breathed an alert vitality that was as strikingly in contrast with the former sluggish fearfulness and timid caution as the April flight of a bird with its huddling search for protection and warmth from the winter wind.

That divine love was and is strong; but, more marvelous to our human hearts, it was constant. It persistently refused discouragement: where gaiety was frowned from the room and serenity mistaken for weakness, the roar of thunder and jabs of lightning were thrown into man's life, to be as readily substituted for by gaiety and serenity. Apparently as changeful as April, it is actually as persistently unabashed in the face of discouraging refusal. There is in it that same ingenuity of effort, that complete unanimity of spirit in all its moods that marks the work of April revivifying earth. For that, after all, is the good which divine love wishes for us; that we might live, might have life and have it more abundantly. And it is this constant will for our fullness of life that explains all the apparent vagaries of God's love, the divine exemplar of April's inconsistent consistency.

It is not hard to see, beneath April's independence, thoughtlessness, youthful disregard of things, a wise understanding, a ready forgiveness, friendly tolerance. And eventually co-operation is won from a sullen, grudging, stubborn earth. Would any other means win such cooperation? Is there anything of April's varied attack on death that could be spared? Is it not rather that, carrying the figure through, April's love of life and of earth is strong enough to be severe as well as deep enough to be gay, solid enough to be serene?

And the same thing is true of the hearts of men in their ultimate response to the April of God's love. When that divine life begins to course through our veins, we discern, always dimly, something of the understanding that spared the adulteress rebuke, the forgiveness that resurrected Magdalene, the toleration that finally made Peter in truth the Rock, the gentle, patient, untiring cooperation that made apostles of fishermen. What is more to the point, we begin to trace those things within our own lives.

In a sense then, except where pagan winter has chilled life to its very bones, Catholic life is a perpetual April; a mixture of serenity, gaiety, thunder, and lightning based on unfailing constancy and strength. The Catholic's attitude toward life, then, is a divine attitude. Having life in its fullness, the Catholic must play April to another dead earth, must filter through its frozen surface all the divine things that have brought his own soul to life. This is the realization of our love's desire to do things for God, as it was the answer to the desire of God's love to do things for us. Perhaps it is true that only those eager for life can enjoy and fully understand April; surely it is true that only the Catholic can fully enjoy and understand the April that divine love has made of human life. Above all, it is strictly true that only Catholic strength and constancy playing through the unpredictable moods dictated by divinity can bring life to the barren hearts of men.

CHAPTER ELEVEN

Four Reasons for Immodesty

OUR AGE has undoubtedly discovered much. It is no less true that it has merely uncovered much more; and sometimes it would be much better if we had stayed away from the graveyard and left the corrupting thing in the quiet oblivion of its grave. There is, for example, the intense concentration of our time on what has come to be called propaganda. There have been uglier names for it in the past; but the point is, it has existed in the past, indeed, as far back as our records go. Our contribution has been to give it wings that might contaminate still more territory.

Propaganda is, in fact, no more than a revival of the satanic device of garbing a vice in the enticing robes of virtue, while the disgusting garments of vice are tossed over the head of virtue. Then the first is paraded before the public as the reigning beauty; and the second is hidden away in disgrace, lest the deception be discovered. To paraphrase a recent *bon mot,* it becomes hard to hate a vice until you know it well; and then it is often too late. Twentieth-century life is crowded with examples of this trickery: political slavery is championed as political freedom, clemency as weakness, meekness is spinelessness, war is a campaign of peace, ruthless aggrandizement wears the smile of unselfish benevolence, and so on.

All that, however, is on a national or even an international scale. We need not go that far afield for an example of this trickery which has been unfailingly successful for untold centuries; that is the diabolical propagandist's display of immodesty in the garments of modesty. As an indication of how deeply this propaganda has penetrated into our thinking, there is the fact that if we were called on to give examples, offhand, of modest and immodest dress, we would mention a nun's habit and a modern swimming suit. As a matter of fact the nun's habit is, on one count, immodest, for it hides from men the human beauty she has dedicated to God. Christian modesty, on the other hand, is a defense and extolling of a woman's freedom and beauty.

All modern publicity to the contrary, this title of defender of freedom and beauty does not belong to immodesty. There are only four reasons for immodesty, and all of them are open enemies of woman's freedom and beauty: namely a desire for singularity, laziness, lust, and a distaste for human beauty. The first has many disguises. Sometimes it is hypocrisy, at others, eccentricity, again it is silly vanity; but whatever its immediate source, at its roots is an utterly humiliating confession of inferiority that fixes its sole hope of attention on the startling character of dress. Laziness may be spiritual or physical; in the first it robes the hypocrite, in the second the slattern. Lust is always hunting fuel for its consuming fire; while distaste for human beauty is the inevitable corollary when men forget that they are men.

The first three are chains enslaving the heart of woman; the last is a disfigurement destroying the very idea of beauty in her mind. The thirst for singularity insists that a woman neglect the one human claim to individual notice, the strictly human and utterly inviolable perfection of the soul by virtue that we describe in a vague way as goodness, in a sharp uncompromising, decidedly uncomfortable way as sanctity. In its place, there is enthroned the entirely extrinsic and utterly frail opinion of others, a monarch of a woman's life that sickens and dies without cause and without heirs. Laziness paralyzes woman's powers, reducing her to the level of a plant's serenely empty vegetation, emphasizing for a time pruning, plucking, and solicitous care, but eventually allowing the plot of her life to go to seed. Lust makes her the slave of the most tyrannous of masters, her animal appetites. They will gnaw insatiably at her very life, destroying what they feed on to a climax of disgust and despair.

But it is the fourth reason for immodesty that receives outstanding attention today: the positive distaste for human beauty. It appears as beauty's champion; but the beauty it advocates is any and every beauty that is not distinctively human. It may be the beauty of a hand, an arm, a leg, a back, or the beauty of hair; the process by which it selects its heroes is a kind of mental dissection that drapes the dismembered body in the window of life like prize beef on a butcher-shop counter, or samples of the mastery of an artificial limb manufacturer. There is nothing uglier than a human being who does not look human, or who is not seen as human. Human beauty does not have to be torn apart, measured, weighed, and scattered over a laboratory table; rather it exists as an inviolable unit because, as human, it is always the beauty of a *person*.

It is precisely this truth that Christian modesty insists upon. Human beauty is the beauty of a *person*. What hides or disfigures the person, hides or disfigures the beauty of a woman, her personal beauty. It is in this sense that a nun's habit may be said to be immodest; for it does strive to hide the personal beauty of the woman who has dedicated herself to the Master whose uniform it is. But personal beauty is a difficult thing to hide when it is being continually developed; it is not surprising that it should shine out from the nun's eyes.

To see a woman as modern immodesty would have us see her, as an animal, a toy, a decoration, demands a grotesque distortion of a woman's personality. It demands that we blind ourselves to the sight of a person with high destinies, fighting heart, cherished dreams, and triumphant failures. The second vision, not the first, is what floods the human heart with the quiet joy that is beauty's trade-mark.

Christian modesty is an insistence on the personal. Beauty is, objectively, the splendor of order breaking through the veil of matter like sunlight streaming through stained glass. It is the rich, full perfection of the soul, an utterly individual thing, lighting up and enriching that to which it gives life. Modesty, as a part of the virtue of temperance, is an insistence that reason's order leave its individual impress on such details as social conversations, games, even on the most petty details of our clothes. It is a demand for beauty in every detail of human life, of the splendor of the soul of a human being streaming through every aspect of this individual human life and activity.

There is little of the attractive about sloppiness because there is little human about it. Personal oddities are not things we admire, but things we tolerate, even oddities in dress, for they are the tidemarks of the inhuman. Hypocrisy we despise, for man was not made to hide behind a mask but to live heartily, sincerely with his fellows. Our distaste for nakedness, whole or partial, is more than common sense protesting against sunstroke or frostbite; we resent the highjacking of love's messenger by the thugs of animality, the desecration involved in tearing away the veil from the tabernacle of the temple of the Holy Ghost.

But the work of Christian modesty goes deeper than the defense of personal beauty to a last-ditch fight for personal freedom. Obviously it breaks down the attacker of oddities, laziness, lust, and love of ugliness. Freedom is distinctively human. A human way of life is a free way of life; and the only human way of life is the life of virtue, the life of driving accomplishment and strong mastery that is the fruit of reason's order permeating the activity that crowds our days. It is in this sense that the nun's habit is eminently modest. It is the arms of one who has enlisted in the fight for virtue's freedom, who has dedicated herself to a fight to the death against the threats, the enticement, the thundering attacks of sin's slavery.

Immodesty is really the activity of one who is ashamed of herself. So she hides herself from the world, refusing to appear before the eyes of men as a sovereign person, an inviolable being, free with the freedom of the image of God, beautiful with the lustrous splendor of divine and human reason. Modesty is not something to submit to restively; rather it is to be championed and defended. And it will need defense. For propaganda has succeeded in making us a little self-conscious about our personal freedom and personal beauty, as it has made us uneasy about such human things as enduring love, fruitful marriage, absolute truth, justice to God, which is called religion, and so on.

In fact, that self-consciousness, that uneasiness, can remain in our lives only so far as we neglect the companionship of the Mother of God. The beauty and modesty of Mary were not miraculous harmonizations of incompatibles; rather they were the normal combination of inseparable things. Modesty is an unveiler of a varied beauty that rivals the splendid diversity of the angelic world, for modesty is the unveiler of the personality of the individual.

It is eminently fitting that May, the tailor of nature, should have been dedicated to Mary. It would demand a particularly perverse mind to see in May the quick gesture of embarrassment covering nature's nakedness. We would have to be particularly blind to see in the beauty of May only the frills of superfluous decoration. We have only to open our eyes to see it as the rich beauty of life breaking forth in the minutest details of nature's garments.

CHAPTER TWELVE

Shortage of Heroes

ALL THE world loves a hero; but there do not seem to be enough heroes to go around. Then, too, one never knows but that a hero would be a very uncomfortable person to live with; he is such a rare person, so utterly different from the normal crowd of men and women that it may be just as well not to come into too intimate a contact with him. At least our age has not raised too loud a protest at being condemned to the dull mediocrity of prosaic routine.

Yet the human heart can never be satisfied with the leaden quality of mediocrity, even though it can find no more nourishing heroic food than that offered by the world of make-believe. It does not do to take the thriving appetite for movies on the heroic scale, detective thrillers, and wildly fantastic pulp magazines too seriously; but then neither does it do to take a starved human heart too lightly. And it is undeniable that today the individual human heart is starved for the heroic. It has only the choice between the anonymous satisfaction of group accomplishment or the vicarious satisfaction of fiction's heroics. Neither gives nourishment enough to a heart made for high, hard things, a heart made for the complete consecration and unquestioning sacrifice involved in love's response to love.

Perhaps no one realizes this more keenly than does the Catholic woman, when, during the month of June, her eyes are focused on the selfless heroism of the Sacred Heart of Jesus. Here is a place for heroism, because here is a place for the bitterly joyous language of love. What the Catholic woman so

often forgets is that her own life is in fact lived on a heroic
scale, that the life of the practical Catholic woman is in solid
fact a response, and a fitting response, to the appeal of the
Sacred Heart.

Apparently she has plenty of evidence to justify her challenge of any such claim. She has daily reasons for discouragement in the unflattering contrast of the utter generosity of the
Sacred Heart and her own petty stinginess. There are the hard,
happy resolutions that seem such a solid part of the brightness
of morning; and the crumbled ruins of those resolutions at
the end of the day or the week or the month. There are Lent's
grim determinations and their slow rusting from exposure to the
tiny things that have such a hold on her heart. Her life seems
to her only a mater of plodding along from day to day through
the colorless mists of petty failures; she is giving God only a
corner of her heart, scattering the rest, like a philanderer, on
hundreds of petty loves.

It is unquestionably, though mysteriously, true that the
human heart gives up trifles with painful reluctance, like a
child surrendering regretfully to sleep; while it sweeps away
tremendous things with recklessness and even gaiety. We will
fight to give over our wills in the victorious surrender of
marriage; the world is tossed out the window in a gesture of
ecstatic joy by the nun taking her vows; persecution serves but
to stiffen our spines, while martyrdom is taken for granted from
the man who grumbled so much about the coal collection. Perhaps it is because the trifles that together strangle our heart
seem, taken one by one, to be no threat to the really big things,
that we are careless even of their most jealous caresses. We do
not find it hard, at least not too hard, to make the big sacrifices
in a moment and adhere to them; but we find its a discourag-
ingly difficult thing to make the little sacrifices for all of a lifetime.

This cherishing of trifles or the calm discarding of them is
a matter of stinginess or of liberality. Even the stingy, in
love, surpass liberality though they lack it. For liberality is
not a test of love. Rather it is a statement of our freedom from

the encumbering arms of beloved trifles. By liberality we remain master even in this Lilliputian kingdom, so that we can put these things aside easily, masterfully, without regret. On the other hand, stinginess means that our heart has been caught by the glitter of the baubles. But it does not necessarily mean any more than that. It does not mean that we refuse to give these things up; it may mean only that their surrender is a regretful, reluctant, joyless thing.

The measure of love is not how we feel about the thing we give up, the twinge, or lack of it, in our hearts at seeing this thing go. The measure of love is the actual surrender. And this is the cardinal point that makes *effective* stinginess impossible in love. We may regret having to give this thing up, we may surrender it with solemn reluctance each time its surrender is demanded. But we *do* give it up. In fact, rather than detracting from the quality of friendship, this very reluctance is an unquestionable confirmation of the depth, the power, the full sweep of our love; for, in its name, we surrender what is dear to our hearts. And that is possible only when something far dearer puts in a rival claim.

Perhaps it was to remind us of this highly important truth that our Lord so stressed the small things in the midst of His surrender of all things for us. This is perhaps why, in the midst of such great sacrifices, the details of these very small things should be so carefully preserved by the sacred writers— that we might understand, in our human way, how constant and profound a thing is His open heart. Compared to the agony in Gethsemane, it was a little thing that the apostles should fall asleep when He wanted the human comfort of their companionship. Compared to what they had come out to do, it was a little thing that the soldiers and the mob carried swords and clubs, that they slunk through the alleys of darkness when they came to snatch Him from the Garden's quiet night; yet He protested these very things. The blow of the high priest's servant made Him break His silence in sharp complaint though no word came from His lips through all the scourging.

But then He was always so careful of fragments: of His power, when the woman touched the hem of His garment secretly only to be made to confess it openly; of affection, in His insistence that the children be given the privilege of His caress; of courage, such as kept the woman taken in adultery standing silent before Him though her accusers had fled and the way was open to either flight or explanations; of trust, as Thomas well knew when the wounded heart was offered to his hand. Not that He was stingy; but that our stingy hearts might see something of the nobility He had given them in spite of their stinginess.

For ordinary, routine, even mediocre Catholic life is a noble thing, far outstripping liberality. Liberality, after all, deals with the small change of life; and we too often part with our trifles reluctantly. But we do part with them at His command. We grumble, groan, fidget, are ashamed and embarrassed; but we are back at His feet again and again with the gifts in our hands. We do give up the Sunday sleep, we do elbow our way into crowded churches on torrid days, we do sit stoically through long, dull sermons, we do kneel down and tell the things that only God can know.

And by those very things we proclaim again and again that He has first place in our hearts. We confirm the momentous fact of our love, confirm it unquestionably day after day. And this means that again and again we have put self to one side to work for our "other self" who has so won our hearts. We do not merely say we love Him; we prove it, prove it to the hilt.

Our reluctance and regret, the fruit of our pettiness, have done just this: they have distracted our minds from the nobility of our acts, from the fact that our lives are a high romance where blows are struck resoundingly, bridges burned in spite of the cost (though not without the cost being counted). The joy of battle, honor, and high surprise is there to be savored; the taste of it all instantly sponges the bitterness of regret and reluctant surrender from our mouths. Thus we can maintain that reluctance only by cheating ourselves of the romance of

Catholicity, the pride of family, the joy of high endeavor. But even then the royal blood triumphs and puts its eternal mark of heroism on our every action.

In other words, heroism is not rare in the twentieth century; indeed it is a common thing, as it has been in every century since the Son of Mary walked among men. It is only in a world empty of Christ that heroes must be few and far between; for only in that world is the individual of no value, only there is he condemned to meaningless routine and skies that hold no stars for his reaching hands. In a world that makes room for the Son of God, men and women walk with the stride of God to the goal of God; they may grumble at the pace and sigh at the height of the goal, but nothing that earth or hell has to offer can stop them.

We respond to the love of the Sacred Heart, though we fail to match that divine generosity, still clinging to our trifles. Yet the very realization of the response we are making, of the heroism of this ordinary life, is itself the broom which sweeps our hearts clean of the dust of trifles. We can be small, in other words, only by forgetting that we are being big; we can be discouraged at our failures only by cheating ourselves of the joy well earned by the routine task of tracing the footsteps of Christ. Our lives can seem dull, routine, colorless only if we glue our eyes to the window that looks out on a world empty of Christ, neglecting the divine Guest for whom we have built the house and whom we entertain faithfully, though sometimes with scant courtesy.

CHAPTER THIRTEEN

Private Wars

ALL THE world is by now familiar with such military fundamentals as the anchors of a line of defense. These pivotal points must be held at all costs. Once they are lost, the elaborate defense mechanisms of the rest of the line are completely useless; the whole line must be abandoned without further struggle and at once. The efforts of years, the cautious planning, the long slow labor, the enormous expense, are all wasted. A cardboard line would be quiet as effective, now that these all important anchor forts have been surrendered.

Viewed from the side of the offense, it is precisely these anchor positions that must be the principal objects of attack. Whether by a direct assault or by an encircling or flanking attack, at any cost these positions must be taken or the defensive army rests in complete security. However it may be disguised, the fundamental attack must always be against these key positions of the defense.

It is more than our heritage from devastating wars that makes all this immediately applicable to the hardy business of Christian living. St. Thomas' description of the life of virtue as a private war is particularly apt. It is a war, this following in the footsteps of Christ, a continual war in which a truce is only another name for surrender, and disarmament is the prelude to slavery. This war is never a quick one; hardly more frequently is it a one-sided war with all the odds on the side of virtue; rather it is usually a nip-and-tuck affair with all resources thrown into the battle, rationing a matter of course, and insecurity the prod that makes alertness the common characteristic of those who would survive.

In this private warfare that engages the lifetime of those bold enough to attempt to follow the Son of Mary, a fundamental attack is that of sorrow; and its objective is that anchor of the defense of the peace of Christ which we call patience. When that attack is successful, the whole elaborate Christian defense crumbles almost in an instant; when that fort falls, surrender has already been made.

It is strange that we have so persistently underestimated the virtue of patience. Certainly our Lord underlined this virtue in His passion in a way that left no doubt about the importance He attached to it. Patience was the bulwark against which the envy, jealousy, and injustice of the leaders of His people smashed and broke in that long night of questioning and abuse. The cowardly travesty of Roman justice tried its strength and failed; on Calvary the jeers of the mob, the insults of the priests, and the physical violence of the executioners were huge waves of sorrow beating at the walls of patience that guarded the soul of Christ, delivering themselves of their fury and subsiding into the unspeakable depths from which they had come, baffled. The women of Jerusalem who wept at His suffering saw His helplessness but missed His strength, an error that He would not allow to pass unchallenged: "Weep not for Me." For not only pity is due the Crucified, but unstinted admiration for His mastery that held the pivotal point of defense inviolate.

To the world Christ came to win, and to the apostles He had chosen to conquer that world, patience was a distasteful thing. It smacked of weakness, flabbiness, of helplessness, unworthy of the strength of a man. That pagan world, like our own, knew only one kind of courage and strength, the kind that rushed out to crush others. It knew nothing of the courage that would sustain a man himself, the courage that would assure his mastery in the face of the attack of sorrow.

Yet the importance of this quieter courage leaps out at us from a cursory glance at the routine day of that obscure individual we call the average man. It is the main defense against the trouble-makers that harass the soul of a man. Many of the upsets of an ordinary day can be summed up in terms of anger, resentment, hatred, injury to others, the desire to "get back at" someone. If these things could be removed from our lives, the battle would be a purely personal one, independent of the sharply abrasive contact with other men: against the restlessness of ambition, the rush of desire, the clutch of fear. For ordinary purposes, the battle would be cut in half. A completely peaceful, that is, an utterly masterful, day would be quite an ordinary thing instead of the totally astonishing experience it actually is.

Our age does not allow us to doubt what results may be produced by the crushing blows that mark the great crises of a man's life: undeserved failure, loss of wealth or position, sickness, death of loved ones are the occasions for despair and that scuttling of human life which is suicide. They are the haunting terrors that inspire desperate efforts of escape, the mad embraces of distraction, the hopeless gestures of surrender. For they are the sorrows too often bigger than the heart of man can endure.

What we ordinarily miss is that, fundamentally, these two —the upsets of an ordinary day and the great crises are the same. The thieves of the peace of our ordinary days make their sortie from the fortress of sorrow. Sorrow has conquered our soul; we become angry, we hate, we hurt. But if sorrow has not conquered, then meekness goes its way unchallenged; love gives no ground to hate, and justice orders the serene interchanges with our fellows. The angry, hating, hunting man is a beaten man; a man beaten by sorrow, stripped of the peace of Christ; the anchor of his defenses has been captured and the way thrown open to the vices that now thunder over the soil of his soul.

In reality there is little mystery in the observable fact of a woman growing under sorrow, for sorrow can make or break the soul. It is easy for us to understand the collapse of the soul under the attack of sorrow. That is the modern world's way of dealing with sorrow: crumbling under it or, what amounts to the same thing, maintaining the pretense that sorrow does not exist. But it is not until a woman learns that sorrow must be faced and conquered that she can ever grow to her full stature. Until such a time, she dresses her life in the absurdly ill-fitting garments of childhood and whiles away her days playing childhood's games with none of the child's grace, beauty, or promise.

The fact is evident. But our world is reluctant to admit its sole explanation. How can the deadening blows of sorrow add stature to the soul of a woman? The encounter with sorrow reduces itself to a matter of faith, of doggedly hanging on. But why should a woman hang on with love over, a family wiped out, honor gone, or hunger gnawing at her very life?

Well, for the Catholic woman, there is her solid faith with its vivid picture of another woman, watching her Son gasp out His life on a cross; then going down the hill alone, unbroken, to live the long years alone. There is the constant memory, which is a part of her blood and bone, of that Mother's Son who went up the hill, after a night and a morning of horror, to hang unbroken until the hours had made their slow journey past His high throne. Both of these tell the Catholic woman the reason that alone makes possible the victory over sorrow. For no one can sustain sorrow unbroken unless a greater good nourishes the strength of the soul. Unless there is a God and a heaven, man must slink from sorrow like a beaten cur; as long as there are God and heaven, no sorrow, trivial or calamitous, need threaten the serene living of human life.

Sorrow's conquest, the strength and peace of patience, should be mysteries to women of a world that does not know God, His Son, His mother, and the enduring life they brought to us. Pity should be a familiar thing in the hearts of Catholic women: not pity for Christ or His mother, not pity for themselves, but pity for the women who must face sorrow and be broken by it because they have no reason for bearing it. Sorrow will find its way into every Catholic woman's life; her heart will feel the stab of sorrow no less keenly than the heart of any other woman. But it is not crushed, as Christ was not crushed though He was killed. Her heart is a strong heart, a peaceful heart. And, secure in its peace, it is a merciful, mothering heart for the women who must meet the common enemy, sorrow, shorn of hope and of defense.

CHAPTER FOURTEEN

Champions of Discomfort

S T. DOMINIC was an uncomfortable sort of person. Indeed, it might be said that he left that characteristic mark of uncomfortableness as a heritage to his children: they were to be uncomfortable themselves and to spend their lives disturbing the comfort of others. For comfort is the mark of the man who has done nothing, or who has done all he has to do, and now has nothing of labor before him. It is inconceivable in a man working at a task that only death will finish; it is an impossible fruit to expect from contact with such a man. An apostle may well be likened to a firebrand tossed into the world; he can never be thought of in terms of a feather-bed or a lullaby.

To give this truth its deserved universality, we may say that a lover is an uncomfortable person, made uncomfortable by his very love and almost necessarily a discomfort to others. For a lover is one who has many things to do, tremendous things, even impossible things, things that are limited only by his love: the endless things demanded by love's effective desire for the happiness of the loved one. In other words, a lover is necessarily a zealot. Love can be satisfied with nothing less than such an ardent flame.

It may be a little foreign to our usual way of picturing the Maid of Galilee to see her in this light. But, in view of her life, it would be difficult not to see her this way if we are to see her as she was; for, surely, it would be hard to picture Mary as a woman who was not completely, unquestionably in love. It would be supremely difficult to find a moment of her life that was not crammed with consecration to the happiness of her Son, a moment when Mary had to "get away from it all" and lavish thought, time, kindness on herself. Her love demanded complete absorption in the care of her Son.

It is of no little importance for us to remember that in a sense Mary never quite finished that work of love; she has bequeathed to every one of her daughters her own task of love, the joyous task of caring for her Son.

To say that Mary's Son still has need of that womanly care is not mere poetic fancy or rhetorical exaggeration. For all the unspeakable clarity with which he had seen the completeness of Christ's triumph and the glorious perfection of the Master, Paul could still speak of the faithful completing the sufferings of the Lord. No such divinely inspired insight is needed to see the necessity for the continual nourishment of the body of the Lord, for lavishing a mother's care on the mystical body of the Son of Mary; yet is that not continuing the work of Mary?

It is not insignificant that women should have been given so early a share in the apostolate: that Anna should have begun to spread the good news while the Savior was still a babe in arms; that Magdalen, the apostle of the apostles at the first Easter, should have been driven by love's desire for accomplishment to give her later years to the eternal consecration of the soil of France. It is not without meaning that the very first to receive word of the coming of the Redeemer should have been His Mother and Elizabeth. Indeed, Mary's care of her Child is at the same time a statement of woman's apostolate and its demarcation. It, too, must be preceded by an intense preparation centered on personal perfection. It, too, will consist essentially in bringing Him to the world and the world to Him. The modern woman, like Mary, will step aside to let Christ do His work. Her work, always an intensely personal affair as was Mary's, will be quiet, unobtrusive, indispensable.

There are obvious reasons why the modern Catholic woman cannot neglect this work of Mary's, cannot refuse to be an apostle. There is, for instance, the obvious claim which mercy makes that food be given to the hungry, comfort to the sorrowful, hope to the despairing, and all the other things the Catholic women possesses in such abundance and which she can share only by bringing others to the feet of Christ. This is a powerful human, as well as divine, motive based on the ability to suffer with others, to see the misery of a life without Christ, particularly the life of a woman; the ability, in other words, to understand why the adulteress, who had to be dragged before Christ, did not run away when she was left alone with Him.

There is, too, the intensely personal motive imposed by the possession of news that is too good to keep. It was entirely understandable, humanly speaking, that Mary should have risen up in haste after the Annunciation and sought out Elizabeth, or that Anna should have sought out all who looked for the coming of the Messiah to tell them the news of His coming. This is entirely understandable, for it was based on an appreciation of what Christ meant to human life, on the realization of the nature of the good which can be shared without being given up.

But the absolutely fundamental motive for continuing this work of Mary goes deeper than either of these two reasons. It is the only explanation of the heroic efforts, the serene constancy, and the perpetual disappointment of the saints, yet it is the common possession of Catholic women, for it is the love of Christ.

That love, like all love, necessarily implies a driving effectiveness, a desire to do good for Him. Of course, we cannot even think of supplying for the deficiencies of an all-perfect God. But God, as though stooping to the demands of our love for activity, made it possible for us to do something for Him, to bring into that mystical body all the souls who wander in the darkness of ignorance or malice. Thus it is made possible for us to satisfy fully the imperious demands of love: not only to love what belongs to our divine Friend, not only to embrace the friends of our divine Friend, but even to work for a kind of fullness and completeness for our divine Friend Himself. We can care for His body, nourishing it, strengthening it, perfecting it.

No other motive explains the consuming fire of the saints. Dominic's zeal outlasted the ten-year refusal of the people of the Midi to listen to his voice. On the grounds of mercy or of the personal necessity of sharing a great secret, their contempt, persecution and mockery would have led Dominic to invoke the Lord's injunction against throwing pearls to swine. He would have quit. But on the grounds of love of Christ he could not quit while he had a breath of life and a spark of love in him. Nothing but this love of the Son of Mary could have driven Vincent Ferrer on until he was a broken old man who stumbled over the roads of Brittany from town to town and summoned his worn-out body to superhuman efforts when it seemed he could hardly keep the flicker of life alive for an hour, let alone make a holocaust of the hearts of a whole people. Nothing less could have made the frail strength of Catherine last until she was thirty-three while she recast the course of civilization; nothing more was needed for Thomas to destroy his prodigious strength by early middle age in the intellectual labors that have protected the centuries since his time from the deadly taint of diluted truth. In fact, it is only in this third and fundamental motive of apostolicity, the love of Christ, that the first two motives of interest and sharing of secrets have any solid basis.

True enough, the ordinary Catholic woman is not called upon for the consuming efforts of such saints as these; but she is not to be denied her share in the work of Mary that is still to be done. Perhaps only in eternity will the apostolic value of routine Catholic life be clearly seen. Yet, even to eyes such as ours, clouded by the smoke and the dust of the world, it is clear that a home, as distinctively different as a Catholic home must be, cannot fail to preach Christ crucified and to preach Him in ringing tones. Even though the intense spiritual activity that goes on within the walls of a Catholic home necessarily escapes observation, it would be strange, indeed, if on its walls there were no memento of the Master, if the mutual relations of its members were not a long record of the unselfishness characteristic of those who are the disciples of Christ, if the wild storms of domestic crises were not soon quieted by that divine command, "Peace, be still": so strange, in fact, as to bring into question the very Catholicity of that home.

The personal life of the Catholic woman is itself apostolic, for it is outstandingly human, strikingly divine; after all, it is Catholic. Of course, its interests will be different; for interests are no more than expressions of the habits of the mind and heart. Its amusement will be different, indeed, from anemic boredom and hysterical silliness; for it is that wholehearted, rollicking rest of the soul that is the soul's best preparation for still more prodigious labors. The work or business that engages so many hours cannot be the deadening draught of routine nor the intoxicating drink of greed or power. Rather that daily labor has the quiet beauty of the craftsman's loving stroke as it shapes the fixtures for a heavenly mansion.

All this is an indirect working at the labors of Mary; great as it is, it is not nearly enough for the daughters of Mary. There is still the direct contribution to be made to the care of the body of Christ by a knowledge of faith, a knowledge not merely of the truth itself but of its significance, its implications, a full appreciation of it. There is a staunch pride in that faith, a pride that does not dodge confession of that faith, that does not shun religious discussion, that is not too timid for religious disagreement. But, above all, there are prayer and the sacraments appreciated and used, not as the last ditch gesture of desperation, but as the most powerful weapons in the hands of a Catholic woman.

Some men, who have not bothered to look at the facts, sometimes protest against the extravagance of foreign missions on the grounds of domestic need. Another man Judas, once protested against the extravagance of love; and he was told to leave love alone. He might well have been told to look at the facts; for love that seeks its own has a famine-pinched family and a neglected house. It is not mysterious that, as apostolicity cools off, religion degenerates. The cooling process is itself a symptom of anemic faith and feeble love. Zeal is an effort of love inseparable from it; in its last analysis, zeal is no more than a defense of what we love proportioned to the depth of that love. In our case, defense means not battering down enemies, but awakening friends; for our zeal defends Christ from the loss of the souls that we can gain for Him.

CHAPTER FIFTEEN

Ingredients of Homemaking

ON A brisk autumn day, to breathe deeply is an easy, pleasant thing. But of course we do not object too strenuously to breathing on all other days. Meditation is a kind of spiritual breathing without which spiritual life is snuffed out by strangulation. It, too, has its ideal moments, though of course it must go on at all moments with the pulsing beat that life demands of its accompanist. Strangely enough, the ideal moments for spiritual and physical breathing coincide: surely October fitted by nature itself to contribute to the ease and joy of meditation. It is the moment between ripeness and decay that is full maturity. All nature stops, before plunging ahead to the starkness of winter's death, as if recognizing the full meaning of the long days of spring and summer.

This is the maturity which finally gives an unconscious recognition of an order which has underlaid countless details. A still greater maturity consciously recognizes order and, what is more, creates order; it not only reads the meaning that is written, it writes a meaning of its own. This is the maturity proper to intelligent beings, a maturity that has about it that same air of quiet fullness, but it is not a momentary splendor between ripeness and decay. Rather, it is a continually growing luster that ultimately breaks forth into the bright light of an eternal vision.

Perhaps no better example of this full maturity was ever more simply given than in the words of the Evangelists. "Mary kept all these words, pondering them in her heart" (when the shepherds came to adore her Son) ; "and His father and mother were wondering at those things which were spoken concerning Him" (when Simeon held the Child in his arms) ; "His mother kept all these words in her heart" (as she went down from the Temple after those three days of anxious search in Jerusalem). From the Gospel story it seems that it was a habit of Mary's to ponder divine things, to wonder about them, to keep them in her heart. We recall, for instance, her years of preparation in the Temple, the prayer that Gabriel interrupted, the serene silence before Joseph's uneasiness. Nor was Mary merely reading the divine meaning in the difficult script of everyday things; she learned those lessons and then incorporated them in the writing of her own page in the book of life.

So it is that all generations have come to call her "Seat of Wisdom," for this is wisdom: to ponder divine things and, in the light of those divine things, to judge of human things, in a word, perfectly to order.

Mary was a wise woman. The Catholic woman, who is her child, is a wise woman, must be a wise woman, for she is essentially a homemaker as Mary was.

Long before marriage becomes a personal problem, and indeed all through life if she never marries, the Catholic woman must make a home in the house of her soul. She is a Martha to the sacramental Christ, with this difference: it is not a passing visit for which she must prepare. The Lord abides in her; she must offer Him a permanent, peaceful haven of complete understanding, generous love, sacrifice, and all the things that go into the make-up of a home.

Leaving aside the supernatural for a moment and concentrating on the purely human, it is an unquestionable fact that home is made or unmade by the woman who is its mistress. We are sorry for the widow left to rear her children alone; but we can, with no unkindliness, limit our pity to the woman herself. But in the case of the widower, we can well be uneasy, also, about burnt meals, broken china, lumpy beds, and originally dressed children. In other words, a womanless house has little of home about it, even physically speaking. Nor does that house fare much better where the woman at its head leaves the home to servants, to spare moments, or simply to itself. Such a house may lack nothing of the material, but still it fails to be a home, for what is lacking is fundamental.

When we remember that peace is of the essence of home, we understand that a home is neither made nor unmade by the solidity of its walls, its palatial furnishings and efficient servants. And that intangible but mighty thing which is peace *is* of the essence of home. Surely the house of a woman's soul that is befouled by sin is no home for Christ, it is no haven for the woman herself; there is a civil war going on there and both Christ and the woman are refugees. This is no longer a home but a place to run away from. In the domestic sphere, bickering parents, sullen, rebellious children, self-centered members of a family who can think only of their own rights, all of these destroy home as effectively as a high-powered bomb. Or, taking it on the positive side, that home must be a place of peace, for it is a place where we can rest, a source of strength, a kind of spiritual hospital where our wounds are bound up and our weary souls comforted. Rest, strength, and comfort are not to be sought amid bursting shells and the rattle of machine guns.

But if there is to be peace in the home there must be order there, for order is a fundamental condition for peace. Nor is this merely a matter of picking up clothes and dusting in corners. It is not a mere matter of avoiding slovenliness, though that minimum of order certainly enters into the question. It is much more fundamentally a matter of long goals plainly seen and persistently aimed at; goals that are savored by the mind, that nestle close to the heart and color the judgments of all family activities.

Consequently a woman who finds other things more interesting than the goals of the family, demolishes the home by neglecting its ends; she makes impossible the serene order that must run through the activities of the household if there is to be peace. Her house now harbors chaos in place of order, and war in place of peace; whatever the funeral hush that haunts its rooms, the perfect service it boasts, the deluxe hospitality it offers to an unceasing parade of guests. For in this household, first things are not put first; they are put out. This insistence on the primacy of first things—long, far, hard things—is at the very root of order and so of peace. Thus it is that, on a purely natural basis, the primary place given to the consideration of the children, their health, their growth, their education, their future, gives an almost automatic peace, for it gives an almost automatic order.

Pushing this thought a step farther, we readily see that peace is the fruit of wisdom, since it belongs to the wise to put things in order. If wisdom is a grasp of the goals and a judgment of all the steps in the race in the light of those goals, if it is a familiarity with the end by which all the means are seen and evaluated, obviously any order less than that proper to the wise man is as shortsighted and risky a thing as passing on a hill. How can we make an intelligent work of today if we have no notion of tomorrow; and how can we prepare and provide intelligently for all the tomorrows unless we know the last of them to which all others point their steps?

There is a literal and beautiful truth in the reward promised in the seventh beatitude: "Blessed are the peacemakers: for they shall be called the children of God." It makes children of parents, and home as wide as the world; which is as it should be. For the Catholic woman is a peacemaker because she is a homemaker. She will be sought, even instinctively, in all the family's search for peace: for physical peace when the children depend utterly upon her in their hurts and sicknesses, for intellectual peace in the midst of the doubts and problems of her husband and her children, for the emotional peace that only love and sympathy can give. Her joy in the homemaking is only another witness to the effects of wisdom at work; for it is wisdom's happy task to turn labor to rest, and bitterness to sweetness.

In the concrete, this means that the closer a woman gets to the last things, the divine things, the better homemaker she is, for the wiser she is. But how to get closer to those divine things? St. Augustine's dictum is still true: we advance toward God, not by steps of the body but by steps of the heart. And Mary's practice is the primary requisite for the taking of those steps; she pondered these divine things in her heart. The parallel, in the natural order, of the Virgin Mother's first step in homemaking is seen in the mother's pondering the things of others, of children, of husband; and it has analogous results, a measure of peace because of its measure of wisdom.

But this is looking at a little world in the light of a partial end, not of an eternal enduring end. It will give a little peace, a kind of home, a degree of order; but not that foretaste of our heavenly home and eternal peace that must be the characteristic of a Christian home.

It is essential to women, then, that they ponder divine things, that is, that they read, meditate, give their hearts a taste of the serenity of quiet prayer. It is not mere chance that women show such a quick appetite for frequent Communion, for daily Mass, that they are often the motive power in the family getting to the mission, and so on. These things hit the very heart of their homes, and women are quick to realize their importance, panic stricken at any evidence of neglect of divine things by the family.

In a family of twelve, where does a woman find time for such reading, meditation, quiet prayer? This is the difficulty naturally brought up by a pagan world which does not understand that this thoughtfulness of wisdom is not so much a matter of a quiet day as of a quiet heart; not so much a matter of closed eyes as of eyes wide open; of using the routine of family life for plunges into the heart of things divine.

With her mind fixed to the last things, the divine things, a woman's little world is seen in the light of the divine; not in the light of social advancement, financial position, conquests of the children, personal convenience, and all the other false beacons that lure the modern home to destruction. The light that illumines the long future of her family is a divine light, the goal of real happiness for herself and her family, the light of the eternal home of which her home is a miniature.

The enemies of the home are the enemies of wisdom, those things that pull the mind and heart of woman away from proximity to divine things, that make it impossible for her to ponder these divine things and, of course, impossible to judge by them. Such things, for example, as the overwhelming interest in earthly things that infests the heart of the mother who has no time for her home. Or, by way of corollary, there is the sluggish lack of appreciation of things spiritual, the jaded appetite's distaste for the things of God; the inevitable enemy that dogs the footsteps of the pagan mother whose eyes fail at the earthly horizon. And then there is sin. The immediate and complete opposition between our very notion of a mother and of a slave of sin is nature's revulsion from the burlesque of homemaking by one who is completely lacking in wisdom, who has made a shambles of her own life, who knows nothing of peace. Vice and the Catholic woman must be strangers, at least they can never be intimate friends; for there is no such thing as a vicious homemaker and the Catholic woman is essentially a homemaker.

Mary was the perfect mother, the ideal for all homemakers, because she was the seat of wisdom; that is, because she was so very close to God, because everything that affected that family circle was seen in the light of the divine goal. There is no other prescription for homemaking, which means there is no other prescription for a Catholic woman's life. Wisdom alone gives order, and tranquil order is peace; without peace, home cannot exist.

Not any wisdom will do, not the light of any goal will suffice to guide the family home: it cannot be an animal wisdom whose goal is the satisfaction of the senses, not worldly wisdom whose norm does not exceed the limits of the world, not satanic wisdom that cannot see beyond the limits of the individual. It must be true wisdom. There is no home in a pig pen, in the uproar of the world, or in hell.

CHAPTER SIXTEEN

Reasons for a Fight

THE TWO moments of Christ's life which stand out most strongly on history's pages are the first and last: Bethlehem and Calvary. In the one He faced life's beginning; in the other, He faced life's end. Neither the beginning nor the end of human life can be faced without courage. Perhaps there was something symbolic in His helplessness in both instants: in the one, the utter dependence of infancy; in the other, the final, agonizing fixedness of a man whose hands and feet are nailed to a cross. In neither case did He run away from life.

It is most important to remember that He could have run; in the last instance, He Himself said He could have twelve legions of angels, as though help were needed for an omnipotent God. Humanly speaking, it was impossible for Him to escape that beginning and that end. New-born infants are as incapable of flight as crucified men. But divinely speaking, the barrenness of the cave and the starkness of the cross could have been escaped. Because He was God, He could have run away; but because He was man, life's beginning and life's end had to be faced.

Since the Son of God lived a human life, millions of men have been called on to face life's beginning, life's progress, and life's end. It has been true of every one of them that, because they were men, they could not run away; if they did fly from life, they sacrificed their very manhood. For, of course, it was not merely the feebleness of the infant nor the nails driven into the cross that made it humanly impossible for Christ to run away; it was the very fact of His manhood. Human life cannot be lived without courage; when that life has been divinized by fellowship with Christ, it is an impossible life for a coward. The cowardice that would attempt to escape the hard things of Christ inevitably cringes before the hard things of human life.

Perhaps no other century has had such need of thinking of Christ's human courage; certainly no other age has had so many reasons for reading the brave old story again and again. The superficial observer may be misled by the physical courage that moves men and women to do heroic things almost nonchalantly in times of war; but only the superficial will miss the fact that the desperate fighting of men comes about from the drive of fear, and will continue under that same merciless lash.

We, of this century, have seen the tactics of the bully paraded undisguised before the eyes of men. We have been indignant, resentful, perhaps frightened in a helpless sort of way. It will be strange if we do not, eventually, realize that bullying is the correlative of cowardice; that it is the cowardice of an opponent upon which a bully grows strong.

That obvious truth tells most of the story of the enfeebled human lives that have slunk through the days of this century, clutching youth, beauty, and security as though these things could be eternally grasped with the fingers of a human hand. To take this whole discourse out of the atmosphere of physical war, it is fairly evident that we have been badly bullied: we have been cowardly, profoundly, and inhumanly cowardly. We have been afraid of life, and the world, making the most of our cowardice, has bullied us.

The modern woman walks the days of her life in terror; in terror of so many and such trifling things that the terror becomes almost ridiculous. Run through the pages of a popular magazine, glancing at the advertisements; you can almost hear the crack of the whip of fear. A woman, unless she continually spends her thought, money, and energy, will, we are assured, be socially unacceptable, lonely, an ogre with rough skin, bleary eyes, and falling hair; her teeth will undoubtedly be lost;

awkwardness, ugliness, and germs dog her every step. She may even, some day, grow old; or, what is infinitely worse, look old. What a life! And this is the least of it.

What mental gymnastics are demanded that truth's solidity be avoided! What brazen masks are prepared that the fiction of irresponsibility may soothe the playful heart! How resolutely the modern woman turns from the finality the human heart demands, lightly shrugging off the inevitables of immortality and death! Home is a beautiful thing if it can be arranged conveniently for a creature who must remain all the long days amusing and decorative. Virtue is a spoil-sport, particularly the lovely virtue of the Lady Mary. And what has a twentieth-century woman to do with a bloody man staggering under a cross on His way to death? Life is filled with emergency exits; more can be built; the coward must have a place to run.

Human life is hard. Human living is a brave thing, not to be measured in terms of convenience, appetite, amusement, or decoration. Because it is human, it is a succession of deliberate choices: of rejections of the inhuman and embraces of the human; of refusal to whitewash evil and of championship (not tolerance) of good. In human living there is no sweetness in compromise, only the bitterness of defeat; there is no solace in appeasement, only the terror of a renewed battle; there is no hope in surrender, only the despair of complete defeat.

Then, too, nature is inexorable. She gives no absolutions from her punishments. Those who will not see become blind; cheating lovers become enemies; the selfish are finally locked in the narrow cell of self; the greedy become misers; the voluptuous, bored; the unjust, friendless. Only those who throw their lives away find them; only those who forget self are enriched.

When human life is raised to the divine plane by God's grace, it is ever so much harder, and ever so much sweeter. There is no theatrical trick by which the rocks of the Garden become roses and its cold moonlight a warming thing. The cross cannot be worn on the shoulder of a gown as effortlessly as you wear an orchid. The revilings of the mob are not turned into the soothing patter of polite applause. Brutes still gather under the cross to "sit and watch." Its shadow still reaches out to the hearts of friends.

But still it is so much easier. For angels walked in the Garden; only under a cross can we walk gayly, even liltingly, in the dark; there is always One to help with the cross and friends to stand loyally beneath it to the end. A rough road is not too much for a woman when it is going some place, particularly to so satisfying a place as a heavenly home. Danger is not more than a woman can face when it does not threaten the things that alone are worth achieving; love is not too difficult as long as it offers opportunities for sacrifice; labor is not too depressing when its every obscure instant is a ringing blow on the gates of an eternal city. And loneliness is an impossibility when Mary and her Son walk the familiar road with the children of men.

Labor and danger are not to be ruled out of human life by an imperial edict, an economic theory, a political revolution, a scientific discovery, or a philosophical thesis. Perhaps that is why human life can be divinely significant in the blood of Christ, humanly noble in Nature's futility, inhumanly despairing in modernity's chaotic meaninglessness. Certainly it cannot be met by hiding among the animals, merging in a mass, or flying to the ends of the earth. It will not do to try to parade in divinity's garments, playing God; to put on brutish masks, pretending we are not men; to play our way through life as thoughtless children. For, you see, we are not gods, not animals, not children, but men. To live the life of men will always be work for the stout heart.

It was perhaps inevitable that an age corroded with cowardice should be sharply challenged to face life or surrender humanity. Cowardice is the nourishment of the bully; and the flight from life, at one time or another, takes a last step beyond which it cannot go. To those to whom surrender of humanity seems the easy, wise choice, the Cross will always be an inexplicable folly. The Cross, after all, was set up as a saving sign for *humanity*; and a Man died on it. Its meaning cannot be read by anything less than a man; the fullness of its meaning will be apparent only to men who lead the divine life instituted by the God-man who wrote the message of the Cross.

For only men understand there are things worth fighting and dying for, even when death will not gain them nor prevent their loss; and only the men signed with the sign of Christ know that the worth while things are never lost by death, never gained by mere clinging to life. Only they have tasted the intoxicating joy of the death that is life.

On Calvary there was one Man brave enough to die and one woman brave enough to go on living; so all men may know that life and death demand the same ingredient of courage. And courage demands the high goals that give ultimate meaning to both life and death. In our time it has finally become unquestionably necessary to face both life and death, and the goal that lies beyond them both. Despite all the hideousness that has forced that decision, ours is an age in which Mary and her Son will be much more at home than in the fear-ridden days that preceded it. The Catholic woman —the intimate of Mary and her Son, familiar with labor and danger and the courage that braves them both, a veteran of the living of divinely human life—is the Mary of our time. Let her slink from life, and how can others hope?

CHAPTER SEVENTEEN

Heart Warmers

LONG AGO, on a winter's night, a man, a woman, and her Child were gathered close in that most primitive of shelters, a cave. Mary and Joseph were there to welcome the gift from on high. Hope lighted that cave, and happiness warmed it; there fear was eternally entombed, and love lifted its challenging voice demanding sacrifice. The Word of God was made flesh and dwelt among men; and the angels of God, with the simplest of men, rejoiced in His coming.

Christmas. During the war years, men, women, and children took to that most primitive of shelters, under the ground. Night after night they huddled together in a fear that still bowed to courage. But despair was never far off, dull resignation numbed the terrors, and steadily mounting hate held horrors for the future. This underground shelter was a means of escaping the brutality that patrolled the skies. Though life could be saved by it, the souls of men were shaken, hour by hour, by the roar of guns and the crash of bombs.

How could the angels' song, ricocheting from the hills of Bethlehem so many years ago, be heard above the din of war? The Christmas anthems are a framework in music for the quiet picture of Mary's serene adoration and Joseph's unquestioning loyalty. But what has music and serenity to do with Christmas? What place is there for the Prince of Peace in a world still mangled by the teeth of war?

As a matter of fact, this is the kind of world that would seem familiar to the Infant of Bethlehem. The quiet of the night in Judea was a cloak hiding the bitter war in the hearts of men; He came to a world of men at war with themselves that He might give them peace. The misery of men called louder to God than the perfection of Mary. He did not come, that first time, to frost the cake of human joy, but to redeem men from the misery into which they had plunged themselves; to that end He Himself embraced misery beyond any seen in the world before or since. A world at war is not a world abandoned by Christ, rather it is a world in which the Son of God walks tirelessly among men, up and down the long roads that men wander seeking the peace that only He can give.

If such an age as ours held only horror, brutality, hate, and destruction, there would soon be no men on the face of the earth. This is too much for the hearts of men to sustain. It is another wonder of divine mercy that in precisely the age where men have heaped the greatest misery upon themselves, where men are obviously brutes, the divine in men is least hidden.

For the misery of others startles man into an unguarded gesture that is characteristically divine.

It is unquestionably true that if the misery of others touches us at all, it does not lay a gentle hand coaxingly on our shoulders. Its grasp is rough, arresting, imperious. Something must be done, and at once. What is more, until life trickles from our fingers, we refuse to admit, whatever the odds, that nothing can be done. It is a startling thing for any man to be jarred into immediate action. It is astounding to the placid laborer, the quiet clerk, the aloof scholar to be suddenly confronted with the rich depths God has buried in their hearts: fighting hearts, undaunted courage, a limitless capacity to forget themselves that others may be helped. It is an amazing revelation to the woman who has been a stranger to violence and into whose very bones have seeped the peace, orderliness and friendliness of home life, to find herself facing unimaginable terrors because a child is in danger, a woman is hurt, or a man is hungry.

We can accustom ourselves to our own pain, our own privation. We may even lose hope and refuse to fight on where it is only a question of ourselves. We cannot accustom ourselves to the misery of others. We cannot abandon hope for them and stand aside, detached, while they writhe in agony. The cry of a hungry child, the agony of a woman, the exhaustion of a man transforms us from average men into heroes of mercy.

If the misery of others does not startle us, then it has not touched us. Perhaps the reason is that we have built a wall about our lives to protect us from such a sight; but by that wall we have also imprisoned ourselves, shutting out love, friendship, the wide gardens that are laid out in the hearts of other men and women. Those who are very proud or very selfish may walk through all of life and never see the misery of others precisely as misery. To their blind eyes this thing is punishment, the entirely just wages of inadequacy, or a mere trifle because these other human lives are mere trifles. But these people barely, on the slender grounds of improbable possibilities, lay claim to the name of men and women in their action; they are the incredibly stupid ones who expect to find fullness of life in a practical denial of God, the world, other men and women for a concentration on the narrow limits of their unpleasant selves.

The gesture of mercy is spontaneous, unguarded. Its very nature, rushing to the help of another in agony, precludes the thought of self involved in the notion of a guarded look, a careful step, a measured word. We cannot be cagey under the whip of mercy; this is not the time to name a commission, to instigate an investigation, or to pass a resolution. It is the time to help. There will be no other moment when such help can be given. It is the moment when the whole past labors of a man surge to the surface in a whirlwind of effective action; or when that man is weighed in the balance and his empty past demands that he be pushed to one side as futile, ineffective, worthless.

In a deeper sense, the spontaneity of mercy is the alert, almost instinctive, gesture of self-defense. For, if we are to work against the misery of others, we must first have somehow merged ourselves into the lives of these others. The merger may be one that has only the physical basis of common experience or common threat, the sort of thing that makes it so easy for the endangered, the old, the weak, the unhappy to be merciful. Or the merger may result from that entirely spiritual bond which is utterly independent of the years of a man's life or the strength of his arm: the common bond of love that makes another's life our own, that enables us to lead multiple lives because we have literally multiplied ourselves in other selves.

The point is that misery calling forth mercy, even though it be mercy based on no more than physical bond, has struck a spark of divinity from the flint of humanity. However dark the misery of men, it never causes a complete blackout in the hearts of men. It is not enough to say that those darkened hearts are cheered by the infinitesimal brightness of a spark; it is closer to the truth to see the darkness of misery illuminated by a soft, steady glow which went unnoticed in the brighter days of carefree happiness, a divine glow that has always lain hidden in the hearts of men.

That gesture of mercy is divine. In God Himself mercy's proper act of supplying the defects and needs of others is the supreme act of His omnipotence. Transposed to accommodate our human range, the sweetness of mercy's music has no such complete perfection; for we are not God. Our perfection does not consist precisely in service to others, in supplying the defects of the miserable; we are not primarily superiors but primarily subjects. We are creatures under God and, like all creatures, our perfection consists precisely in that subjection.

In fact, this could be put more strongly by saying that it is only in proportion to our subjection to God that we can effectively produce the act of mercy which is so distinctively the act of a superior. This is another of those endless paradoxes emphasized by a God's becoming man: only in being subject can a man act as a superior. Yet, on the face of it, it should be obvious that only as a man approaches the likeness of God can he, even in small human things, take on the role of God. In other words, only as he perfects himself can a man minister to the imperfection of others.

If the mercy that misery brings into action springs from the spiritual bond of love, then indeed does it light up the darkness of man's lives with divine light. It was, you remember, divine and human love that warmed and lighted the cave in Bethlehem. Indeed, it was love behind the sweeping omnipotence of God that furnished the bonds which tie together mercy's great works: creation, Bethlehem's joy, Calvary's sorrow, and the enduring peace of the Eucharist. The gap between Bethlehem and Calvary is easily bridged for us by the footsteps of a Man who was God; but the gap between creation and the uncomplaining presence on a lowly altar is no less easily bridged by the insight into a divine love that made God one with us and made us one with God.

Taking the world in a larger sense, it was the misery of nothingness that called forth the divine *fiat*. It was the misery of pagan despair as a climax to sin that called the Son of God to live among men. It was the misery of sin and bleakness of hardened hearts that sent the Son of God to Calvary with His cross. It is the misery of lonely hearts that moves the divine Friend literally to take up His abode on the altar. Throughout the whole magnificent story our misery became God's in the sense of an imperious call to immediate action.

The night of the first Christmas was fearfully dark, so dark that in all the world the only pinpoint of light was the mercy of God hidden in the cave of Bethlehem. Men were much closer to despair then than they can ever be since that first Christmas passed into history. The cave of Bethlehem was quiet, serene, thick with the drowsy peace of home; the caves of war trembled with the reverberating power of the bombs, shrapnel rained on the ground over them, the skies above them were torn with rapiers of light stabbing the darkness in search of a machine of death. In these modern caves there were men, women, and children huddled together with strangers in a security that has no resemblance to home. There was misery in the modern cave, profound misery. And because there was misery, there was divinity and the light of divinity shining through the hearts and minds, the eyes and arms of men.

How can we say that the Christmas of any age or of any year is bleak or lonely if we limit our eyes to a search of the surface of men's lives? Christmas was not a mere matter of a quiet cave in Bethlehem: it was more importantly a matter of a man, a woman, and a Child who was God; still more importantly, is was a matter of the hearts of that man and woman, the divinity of that Child. The quiet reaches of the human heart persist under the roar of the planes and the thunder of the guns. There is still peace on earth to men of good will. The chant of the angels still finds its echo in those who brave the darkness of the night serene in the promise of God.

There is happiness still; but happiness that is much deeper than the depth of a cave, much longer than the days of a life, much higher than the skies from which the bombs rain. Christmas of today, as of every age, is the Christmas in which the misery of men opened their eyes to the presence of God; Christmas of today is the Christmas in which the misery of men called most loudly for the mercy of God. It will, perhaps, be our joy to live to see the full answer to that call.

CHAPTER EIGHTEEN

Simple

THE WORLD situation has so completely occupied the minds, and so the tongues, of men and women in America that it is only with difficulty that one catches the undertone of other things in the hubbub of political unrest. But here and there, in the slack intervals of international discussion, a complaint is heard more and more persistently. The burden of that complaint is the complexity of modern life.

This protest is not so much a whining plaint as one of slightly bitter irritation. So many things have to be read (newspapers, magazines, books); radio programs that we must hear; cars, houses, and clothes that we must own; things to do and places to go. Life is moving at such a pace that several things must be done at one time: food must be taken on the road, conversation made in the midst of a radio program, books and magazines read in digests as we whirl along. Finally it becomes too much even for our energetic age. The good old times come in for a more emphatic mention; the horse-and-buggy days when an evening at home was not a symptom of misanthropy, when a stroll did not indicate the loss of a car or threatened bankruptcy. These were the days when men had time to think, to love, to live.

Much is wrong with this nostalgic picture. In those good old days, people reported for work at seven o'clock and worked until six, if the day's work was light; moreover, they worked six of the seven days. In the spare time thus afforded there were such chores as baking, dress-making, carpet-sweeping, and curtain-stretching. Our leisurely five-day week and eight-hour day, not to mention the speed of our travel and the labor-saving devices of home and office, would make our ancestors snort at our complaint of the complexity of life.

Certainly it is not that we have less time than a previous age. If anything the pace of our lives suffers in comparison with the body-breaking activity of a Vincent Ferrer, the ceaseless labor and travel of a Thomas Aquinas, the hectic activity of the Mendicant Friars in that century that we insist on drawing in leisurely lines. It is not that we have more to do, or that we have less time to get it done, or yet that we have less help in accomplishing our tasks rapidly; rather all the contraries of these statements are true.

The complaint centers properly not on the complexity of life but on our bewilderment with it. We should like life to be much more simple, as a child would wish a jig-saw puzzle to have fewer pieces. What we have mistaken for the increasing impediment of complexity is really the frightening increase in the evident absence of order in our lives. It is not that life has so many more pieces, but rather that we know less and less what to do with the individual piece that is put in our hands. Human life cannot be simplified. In fact, simplicity in human affairs has richly earned the opprobrium formerly attached to it; whereas it deserves none of the home-sick desires it awakens today. In the world of things as they are, simplicity is not something to boast of; it is an absence of perfection. Even the Lord Himself did not advocate unquali-fied simplicity; He put it: "Be ye therefore wise as serpents and simple as doves."

Human life cannot be simplified without being stultified. Human life is, by definition, a period of perfective action, action perfective of body, mind, and heart. It is not merely an incidental fact that man's physical make-up is more complex than that of an amoeba; as we go up the scale of created beings we also go up the scale of complexity, for we go up the scale of potentialities and of their fulfillment. The simplicity which is perfection is so divine a thing that it can be approached only by the artistry of sanctity.

Such simplicity is necessarily uncaused, absolutely first and completely perfect; here obviously we are talking of divinity and of divinity alone. Whatever is caused, and that means all other than God, is necessarily complex, at least with that complexity of a nature proper to it and an existence that is borrowed from infinite existence. Even though it should have no greater composition than this, a composite thing is in some sense after its parts; so the completely simple being must be first if it is to be simple. And it must be absolutely perfect if it is to be absolutely simple, for imperfection is only another word for a star still out of reach, a hole in the fence, or a wall that shuts off the rest of the world.

Highly metaphysical and abstruse as this may sound, it is implicitly grasped by every man and woman. The simplicity we admire in the human world is not simplicity at all but the appearance of simplicity; and it is our ability to detect the artistic achievement of that appearance of simplicity that awakens admiration within us. Does any woman imagine that the richly simple gown which focuses all eyes on itself is the product of a fumbling peasant seamstress who knew no better? The limpid simplicity of style, say of Stevenson, is separated by a long hard road from the complexities of the high school sophomore's essay. The easy familiarity and clarity, the obvious simplicity of a radio talk by President Roosevelt was not the product of naivete. The economy of lines in a master's madonna and the economy of notes in a master's symphony are prime examples of the sublime in the artistry of making the complex look simple, sound simple.

All these things, from the gown to the symphony, have the appearance of easy naturalness, almost as though they were dashed off in a first effort, almost as though they had caused themselves. There you have it: the appearance of being first, uncaused, and completely perfect. The image of divine simplicity shining through the complex efforts of men and women. Obviously these things are not so simple as they look; they are the products reserved for genius. Behind all of them there is an historical record of time, sweat, unspeakable fatigue, and often enough, tears. Not even genius dashes off these "simple" things effortlessly.

All of this holds just as true of what men do with their lives as it does of what men do with the material that is delivered into their hands. To give a human life the appearance of a simplicity that wins the tribute of admiration from men is a work of consummate artistry. True, such a life has the appearance of easy, unstudied naturalness, of wholesome perfection not striven for but possessed almost unconsciously and from the beginning. The simplicity of a child and that of an old woman telling her beads as she listens for the cautious step of death are really only distant relations; for the child has just started to work on the material of life, while the woman has finished her portrait. The one is the simplicity of unachieved goals, the emptiness of one standing impatiently on the threshold of the fullness of life; the other is the appearance of simplicity wrought by the careful labor of long years of achievement. We love the first, and patronize it; we admire the other, and salute it.

We do not achieve this artistic simplicity of life by knowing less of things; by having less to do or more time to do it in. It is not a thing possible to an age that had straw in the bottom of a carriage and impossible to an age accustomed to the warmly cooled air of a streamliner. It is not accomplished by hiding from men, emptying our heart, letting our hands droop idly in our lap, or by setting a determined mileage for our feet. It is part of the modern heresy to suppose that if we have time enough, quiet enough, and idleness enough the complex components of human perfection will somehow come together of themselves and form the perfect pattern which we call, admirably, simplicity. This is an adaptation of that evolutionary madness which protected us from the terrifying labor of thinking about God and which is now expected to protect us from the also terrifying labor of the living of human life. Of course it will not work. To achieve this artistic masterpiece of human living we must pay the artist's tribute of time, labor, sweat, and tears; the tribute demanded by the task of building up the ramparts of faith, hope, and love, of justice, courage, and restraint. These things do not come easily; nor are they lightly defended. For they are human things with a flavor of the divine in them.

The artistry involved is the artistry of sanctity. Perhaps that can best be seen by understanding our modern bewilderment in the face of life's complexity. A broken string of pearls is a nightmare to a hurried, tired maid instead of the simple, beautiful thing it should have been. A riot of madly clashing colors, with none of the harmonious blending of a rainbow's variety, can drive a man insane if he is forced to stare at it long enough; he can surfeit his eyes with a rainbow's complete array of color and be the better for it. The complexity of things is not what bewilders and betrays man, but their lack of order: the string is broken, and the pearls scattered over the floor. Sanctity's job is to put the splendor of order in the unpredictable variety of the simplest of human lives.

Sanctity makes life look simple; in fact, it makes of life a complex reflection of the divine simplicity. And it does this by the intelligent process of putting first things first. Sanctity aims above all at God, at the vision of Him, the embrace of Him for all of an eternity. Every detail of life fits smoothly into that program or is ruthlessly discarded. The amazing thing is that sanctity can make such good use of so many unpromising details of a human life. Sanctity has a goal, a supreme goal of life, so life is an ordered, smooth, beautiful thing that looks simple.

But what if a man has no goal? What if he knows no God, or at best a God who is far from the supreme goal of his life? Because he is human, his life will be complex. The harder he works at the task of living, the more complex that life will become; the closer he comes to making his life successful, the greater will be its complexity. If he tries the other tack and runs from life, abhors its labors, dodges its activities, shuns its relationships, and denies its responsibilities, it will be terrifyingly complex; for within his very self there is always an intellect reaching for the absolute in truth, a will stretching out for the supreme in good, and animal appetites in a perpetual challenge to the unquenchable flames of intellect and will. Human life cannot by any expedient be made simple. But it can be given the artistic simplicity of human perfection, a simplicity not bewildered by complexity but delighted in it as in so much richer material with which to work.

Our age is not an age that lives too fast, that has too much to do, or too little time to work in. If all these things were changed, modern bewilderment would be no less. For that simplicity which is so divine a thing that it can be approached only by the artistry of sanctity is not to be achieved by negations but by ordered labors to goals worthy of the labor.

CHAPTER NINETEEN

Contentment is for Cows

IF THE rumors are true, contentment seems to work wonders for cows. That should not necessarily recommend it to human beings. It helps, of course in the physical sphere of human life; at least a woman does no damage by being contented with her hair, resigned to her face, and only moderately self-conscious of her appetite. But when she begins to be contented with the uncrowded condition of her mind, the degree of her love, the perfection of her virtue, she has already gone into a process of decay.

These things are never finished, never fully mature; to be content with them is to tuck in the children and move in the furniture before the roof is up, satisfied that the walls will do the trick ordinarily reserved to a completed house. In such distinctively human things as thought, love, and virtue the life of man is a perpetual motion that stops only when death puts an end to the ripening process of human perfection. This is something to be proud of, for it is nature's tribute to the far-reaching limits of human potentialities; yet, at the same time, it is something to be faced with considerable courage, for it means an assignment to unceasing labor.

This is not to be misunderstood as a salaam before the god of progress, that voracious monster which consumes the things that is progressing and pretends that this result of a stout heart is as devoid of substance as yesterday's smile. This modern adoration of progress does not spring from desire to get something done but from the queer urge to be doing something, just for the sake of doing it, as a woman might, if she lived long enough, wear out her face by ceaselessly rubbing make-up on it for the sheer joy of the cosmetic process.

Perhaps it was a haunting knowledge of human limitations that made these modern apostles of progress for its own sake so eager to overlook the fences that hem in every created perfection. If there were no fence, perhaps man might sweep on to the height of divinity; but, by the same logic, there was no barrier separating him from the animals. Both conclusions have been drawn with results that confound intelligence: man is an animal; he is the god of the universe, if it has any god; and progress is not edging up to the higher fence, human progress is not an approach to the boundaries of angelic perfection, it is merely progress with no definite purpose.

It is hard to start with a fund of error and reap profits of truth. This modern dogma certainly started with a fund of error, for it rejected the fundamental truth that gives meaning to the whole whirl of activity in the universe, the truth that God's is the only perfection without a fence around it.

Certainly created perfections have fences marking their limits. We cannot even mention a particular created perfection without stressing its deficiencies, a condition which, if it existed in the social world, would make life a grim thing indeed. In this case we are not being catty; we just cannot help ourselves. If we speak of a "perfect gown" we have, by that very fact, pointed out that we cannot eat it, ride it, talk to it, feed it; it is no help at all in a free-for-all fight, it will not keep our hands warm and may, possibly, frighten the children. Our innocent mention of a "perfect rose" is, at the same time, a denial to the rose of an oak's strength, a sunset's variety, and a child's incessant motion. When in a burst of unselfish praise we hail this man as a "perfect man" we broadcast to the world the fact that this creature is a good deal less than an angel and infinitely short of divinity. If Mary had saluted Gabriel as a "perfect angel," it would also have meant that this celestial visitor was only an angel.

You see, there is nothing in the world that *is* perfection, though this or that thing may *have* considerable perfection. We cannot link perfection to anything, any person in the world without qualifications that distinctly limit perfection. It is as though the world of creatures approached a fountain of perfection, each carrying its variously sized cup. None could carry away more perfection than that cup would hold. No one thing or person has the whole of perfection; each has his proper share of it. A man possesses human life, a thing quite different from animal life and angelic life; none of these possesses life itself. We speak rightly of an angelic intelligence in an awed tone; we cannot speak of an angel as intelligence itself. In a way you might say that the dog that has been trained to go for the evening paper has, by his training, been given a share in human intelligence; so a man by his birth has been given a share (the human share) in intelligence itself.

In a sense, these shared perfections that surround us in the world of reality are complementary parts of a whole pattern. Gathered together they present us with a spectacle that leaves us breathless in admiration. The mind that has taken to itself the colors of autumn, the fragile beauty of clouds, the peace of night, the grace of a bird, the surrender of love, and the sharp, penetrating insight of thought must be either admiring or blind. In each thing, as in each man, we can see something lacking; in the moral order, that is the reformer's spur, since he is so secure in his own perfection. We can see unrealized potentialities that cry out for fulfillment; that is the incentive of the apostle, the saint, the idealist. We can see, too, progress toward a degree of perfection; that, too often, instead of being the grounds of hope is the goad of the modernist blinding him to the fences that limit progress, or even to the things themselves that should be perfected by progress.

Yet all these breath-taking perfections of the world and of men cannot be blended in a blur of progress; the whole they constitute has no organic unity about it. The fences are still up and they will stay up; indeed, the very fact of those fences is invaluable. It gives us a faint hint of a fenceless perfection, as the bleak light of dawn gives a hint of sunlight; it gives us an inkling of richness, a faint silhouette of a Being whom so many-sided a reflection so meagerly portrays.

The moderns' mistake is far from modern; it is as old as Pythagoras and older; as old as the earliest materialists. The modern has brushed aside the goal of things and the cause of things, leaving only the material from which things are made. Without a maker, without a reason for the making, with only the stuff of making left, it is impossible to conceive of a fence-less perfection, a divine perfection that is limitless. For, as a matter of fact, if we argue from the purely material, then every beginning is a sadly imperfect thing, as imperfect as a broken seed or an embryonic child; from this point of view every completion has behind it a story of imperfect beginnings. But this is not the whole story; for the stuff of the world is not the whole story of the world.

The modern has divinized the world, denying limitation to its possibilities; he has destroyed divinity by insisting on a struggling God or by making God out of a struggling cosmos, a struggling individual, a struggling race. Holding only to the material, he is incapable of the concept of a Beginning that never began, of a perfection that was not a completion, of One who *is,* not *has,* perfection.

The modern, then, is confused when faced with the question of progress and perfection. And God knows he has a right to be confused. As a companion in his confusion he has the apostle of contentment and security. The first is involved in the impossible position of worshipping progress that could not start, of facing perfection that cannot be explained, of tearing down fences and denying the fenceless, of denying divine perfection and destroying created perfection. The soft-spoken champion of contentment and security collides with the difficulty that a man cannot merely chew the cud without gagging on it, he cannot just vegetate without going to seed.

The ideal of men as contented as cows while life whizzes by them has no explanation but that of laziness, which is to say the explanation of fear. The exaggerated ideal of idolized progress is somewhat more understandable. At least this confusion could have arisen from the attempt to weigh God in human scales, from the hopeless attempt to picture the perfection of God. It might have arisen in the mind of a man enraptured by the beauty of perfection before his very eyes; that was what betrayed Satan. More likely, however, it was due to the first mistake, pride's insistence on measuring all things, even divine things, with a human yardstick.

It simply cannot be done. We can see clearly that a cause must possess all that it gives to its effect, and much more fully than the effect. We can prove absolutely that God is the cause of all that is. But, when we try to put together the smile of a mother, the power of a tornado, and the fragile perfection of old china, what have we? These things will not fit into one picture. In a way it is odd that we cannot see the parallel between the human and the divine craftsman. We are quite willing to admit that the order to be found in the precise workings of a watch can be, must be, present in the mind of the watchmaker without his head being crowded with timepieces. Why can we not see that the perfections of the world can be, must be, present in a higher way in the divinity from which all things came? We can understand this; we cannot picture it. The attempt to concoct such an image is as hopeless as it deserves to be.

The hopelessness of that attempt is not a reason for casting aside hope. It is not an excuse, for the irrationality of slaying the singer, that we wish the more exclusively to enjoy his high notes; nor of forgetting the singer and distorting his notes that we may escape the double burden of admiration of the song and the singer. Destruction of divine perfection will not leave us more free to concentrate on human perfection; it will destroy human perfection. The neglect of God and the relegation of man to the sphere of plants and animals, the sphere of contentment, will not give us more but less of perfection.

The point is that there is no reason for the hopeless attempt to slap all the colors of the world on one canvas in an attempt to achieve a portrait of God. But there is very great reason for seeing every sparkle of perfection in men, women, and things as reflections of the precious gem of divinity; obviously, if the contact with sanctity, the heroism of sacrifice, the smile of forgiveness, the consuming glow of love can so move and satisfy our hearts, it is worth our while to penetrate behind all these to their infinite prototype.

We wander through the world as a man saunters through the long years of marriage. Day by day, as love deepens and serene understanding increases, he learns more of that eternally mysterious beauty that is another human soul. A gesture here, a word there, a smile, a moment of silence, a stray glance, are revelations of more profound depths, and warnings that the bottom will never be sounded. Just so the years of life roll by and the world passes in review before our eyes, its arms heavy with the treasures it possesses: the coloring of a bird's wings, the fragrance of a flower, the flame of indignation, the ingenuity of craftsmanship, the trust of a child: everything reveals a new depth, otherwise unsuspected, opens up a new vista, gives a novel perspective of the limitless perfection of God.

CHAPTER TWENTY

Pots of Gold

THERE IS a mysterious call ringing through the universe like the challenge of a trumpet. In answer to it there are the entreatingly outstretched arms of trees, the flutter of wings, the pounding of feet, the flailing of arms, the flurry of hearts, the swift parry and thrust of thought. No life is too small, too weak, too humble to join the rushing cavalcade that responds to that call. Some trudge along blindly, unlovingly; others are not blind, but they are unseeing and unloving; while those who run fastest have eyes and mind open to the vision that their love embraces. This is the call that builds factories, lays out blue-prints, fights wars, and puts the finishing touch on the sanctuary which is called a home. It is the first and last sound that rings in the ears of a man; its promise is the first and last thing a man's eyes fix on; the first and last thing his hands reach out for. During most of a lifetime, or even all of a lifetime, it is just beyond the tips of his grasping fingers. It is the call issued by the desirable thing which men call *good*.

Men may be disillusioned, cynical, or suspicious of the good; but not discouraged. In fact, there is hardly any other disillusionment that has been so plainly reflected in language. In its milder forms, the good may be described as the desirable or attractive; but when its appeal reaches the dangerous stage where it threatens to tear the heart out of man, all our descriptive words have an edge of bitterness, of malice, or at least of sly trickery. Then the good is a lure, a bait, a charm, a temptation, an enticement, a decoy, or a siren; love is blind, innocence is naive, sophistication is a bore, sin is disgusting. Fortune is fickle, fame is a lie, power is fleeting, and heaven is far away. So it goes on. Men are cynical, but not discouraged. The whirl of the world goes on, and the goal of it all is never changed; the pot of gold at the end of the rainbow, happiness over the hill, peace after the war, and ever afterward full, happy life. The desirable thing is behind it all, the desirable thing called good.

The suspicion and cynicism of men about goodness, coupled with their ceaseless activity, are by no means disturbing signs, but heartening proof of high goals and vigorous life. There will be ground enough for worry when men begin to stagnate, huddled on a bank of a stream in tears, pitying themselves instead of breasting the current of life; or when they are satisfied with the flotsam that is washed up at their feet. As long as they strike out boldly, the cynicism is superficial; they still cherish the dream that keeps men alive, the dream of the desirable thing. As long as they are suspicious, disillusioned but still searching, they have not surrendered the dream; rather they have kept it untarnished and will take no clumsy substitute for it.

In fact, disillusionment must be a frequent thing since the very nature of man insists that he make three high demands of the good he seeks; very seldom will he find these three conditions fulfilled when he holds the object of his desires in his hands. The first of these demands is for complete integrity. A corrupt fruit, a blasted tree, or a diseased animal awakens no possessive instincts in a man. In the human world, where moral as well as physical goodness is in question, physical integrity with moral corruption may be material for amusement, for contempt, for pity; but not for love. Physical defect accompanied by moral integrity is often lightly dismissed, and rightly so; it is a fleeting shadow on a priceless pearl. When both physical and moral integrity are gone, there is little left to catch the eye of the hunter for the desirable thing; only charity's mantle is wide enough to cover the diseased body and soul of a woman who saw love's acts as a game or a business. In plain language, men are not to be enraptured by the secondhand, the corrupt, the common, the beauty worn thin by much handling.

Nevertheless, this fastidiousness is a discerning thing. It is a difficult, often an impossible, business to repair physical damage; it is not often that such repair does not leave a scar. On the other hand, moral repair is an affair of a moment of penance that re-creates rather than repairs; not infrequently it improves on previous prefection, adding a sweetness, a humility, a solidity springing from sincerity and honest self-appraisement. The soul of Magdalen is not disinguishable in heaven by the scars that sin carved and penance obliterated.

Over and above integrity, men demand that the good thing they seek shall have fullness, maturity. Perhaps this demand springs from a conviction that only such fullness will give peace and the quiet of goals achieved; certainly it alone makes the fruit worth the picking, a treasure to fill empty coffers. Yet, in the physical order, this moment of full maturity—and it is only a moment—is a delicate one. It is the last instant before decline, the moment of ecstasy that immediately blends into satiety and distaste; it has about it an air of fatality, a hush of dread expectancy like the fullness of summer's growth or the exhausted bough about to loose its grip on the ripe fruit. Its lush beauty has a promise of bitterness and disillusionment. Spiritual maturity is, of course, not an affair of a moment but of an eternity. It is not so much a bursting fullness as an expanding capacity; it is a promise of doors opened wider, steps that are longer and faster, truths that are deeper, and love that is higher. It is not a still moment of climax, but an intense fire that feeds on its own heat, a fire that reveals no more of its mysterious capacities except that it will grow hotter still. As there is no end to the appeal of this fullness, so there is no quenching of the thirst for it, no measure of the efforts expended for it, no counting of the steps in the long chase.

Man's third demand of the desirable thing is that it shall be not only full but fulfilling. It must close the gaps in his own perfection, patch up the holes, bring the missing gifts, and awaken the unknown powers. Ultimately it must fill the gaps of nature itself, giving a man an escape from that state that was not good for him from the beginning, the state of being alone. So the desirable things that come closest to man's high demands allow him to multiply his life, to lead multiple lives, to lead the lives of others, even the life of God. In other words, the desirable thing that galvanizes the world into action must not only be whole, of ripe fullness, it must do something for us, to us, with us. It cannot leave us delighted but detached, as before a great painting; it must reach into the depths of our soul, remold our heart, color our eyes, inspire our tongue, and unchain our hands that they may be free. If it does none of these things, we brush it aside in distaste. The desirable thing must fulfill its smiling promise of happiness; it must be a goodness that opens arms of welcome, not one that smugly and sterilely hugs itself.

Obviously, in men, activity, the relentless search for the desirable thing, is not a matter of being driven by an inner force toward a goal that is never seen, or seen only vaguely. Rather the desirable passes at a distance and catches the eye of a man. If it be tawdry, with little to recommend its choice, it may hypnotize its victim with a dazzling smile, be not at all reluctant brazenly to parade what charms it has. But if it be well worth the life-blood of a man's heart, it may hide its worth beneath sorrow, labor, contempt, a cross, knowing full well that, to one who has discerned its worth, all these will be counted as a trifling price to be paid for a boon beyond price.

All the world is crammed with good things. Man, wandering its ways, looks about the physical world like an opulent child, bewildered, paralyzed by an abundance of gifts too great to permit of choice. He grabs at this and that, trying at the same time not to lose hold of all else; and, forced as he is by nature to apply the norm of integrity, fullness, and fulfillment, he casts off one toy after the other in a growing bitterness and suspicious cynicism. If he is fortunate, the toys will begin to lose their bright, beckoning look, and he will raise his eyes beyond the physical to the less tangible, but harder, more enduring, more desirable things of the moral and spiritual order.

Here his disillusionment will not arise from the obvious worthlessness of a pietistic smile, sickeningly sweet, nor from the hypocrite's praise of self through the censure of others; it will not be the ghastly pallor of minimum virtue that gives him a turn, nor the limp handshake of cautiously mediocre virtue. These things can ensnare only the blind. It will be precisely the worth-while things that will leave him unhappy, with a sense of empty-handedness and futility. He will see loyalty, nobility, devotion, courage, friendliness, and all the rest on all sides of him, in the thousands of men and women who pass through the revolving doors of his eyes into his soul: all so worth-while, yet none completely so; each much too valuable to be passed by, yet none so desirable as to erase the vision of the others. Even when he reaches the heights of the robust, heart-satisfying violence of love's surrender, there is so much more to be desired, there is so much lacking in this most precious thing. Really, his position is not so very different from his bewilderment, tireless greed, and ultimate disgust in the physical world. Here, too, he would like to gather all the scattered sparks of goodness that decorate a dark world by their dimness into a roaring flame that would light up that world.

It may eventually dawn on him that these good things must be gathered together to be seen separately, that the spark away from the flame is dead almost as soon as it is alive, that such a variety of desirable things is scattered over the world, not that we might painstakingly pick them up, but that we might, open-mouthed, wonder where they came from. In a word, he may begin to see that no one of these desirable things is to be cast aside in disdain; for each of them bears a divine resemblance. Everything and everyone in the world looks something like God; everything and everyone is striving with meticulous, concentrated effort to improve that resemblance. At least it is clear that every effect has something of its cause about it: the essayist's prose, the poet's poem, the sculptor's stroke, the musician's notes, the father's children, are all faithful miniatures of men. So the divine craftsman, whose name is too big for a universe, scrawled unmistakable initials over the face of the world; signing with grace for His beauty, with strength for His power, with delicacy for His thoughtfulness, with gentleness for His mercy, with stubborn perseverance for His eternity. The divine model was not to be squeezed, intact, into a miniature, or into a million miniatures; but no one thing missed tracing something of that divine goodness without ceasing to exist. From this divine sun, the irresistibly attractive light of goodness has gone out, getting dimmer and dimmer as it penetrated down through lower and lower natures; but wherever is found the mysterious quality that catches the eye and uplifts the heart, there is a glimmer of the attractiveness of divinity.

For, you see, it is God that is the first principle of all goodness: its exemplar, its cause, its end; its model, its craftsman, its goal.

Man's suspicion of goodness is really his own fault. He has read the wrong motives into all the desirable things of the world; they were not trying to coax him into their arms with their smiles, they were encouraging him to keep going in the same direction, but far beyond them. His cynical disillusionment is the result of his own misunderstanding of the very nature of created goodness; it was not meant for a resting place, but for a signal, it is not an inn, but a signpost. He has spread the good things of the world on the floor of his mind, as a man would spread a huge travel-map on the floor of his room; and then, because crawling over the roads marked there gave him none of the joys promised by travel, he has been disappointed, cynical, complaining.

Of course, his thirst for the desirable thing remains unquenched; of course, it will remain unquenched until divine goodness is reached. That driving desire for the desirable thing called good is not to be satisfied with this or that good, but with all good, with divine good. It is a kind of blasphemy to picture the good God in a pietistic fashion; as saccharine, aloof, delicately afraid to step down from the holy card. It is solid truth to see the good God as hearty, vigorous, intense, brimming with full life that enlivens all it touches. It is not irreverence but

penetrating vision to see in God's goodness an allure, an enticement, a desirability and attractiveness almost bold in its insistent
appeal to men. This is the mysterious thing behind the whirl
of the world; this is the beauty that has caught the eye of the
universe; this is the unreached treasure to which all a world
races: the attractiveness of God.

CHAPTER TWENTY-ONE

No Lonely Lanes

FOR ALL the millions of men who walk the face of the earth, there are still many lonely places in the world. There are deserts as empty as a winter sky, jungles as gloomily inhospitable in their riches as a miser, frozen spaces as cold as a bitter heart, former homes of forgotten kingdoms, their luxurious beauty exhausted and bedraggled by the thoughtless tread of many generations and now left alone in their poverty. For the most part, these empty spots on the earth's surface glare sullenly back at the day that lights up their emptiness and wrap themselves gratefully in the nights as in the arms of an understanding love.

In reality, they are not lonely until a solitary man invades their silence and knows he is alone. For it is not places but men that are lonely. Only men can drink down the living water of society, taking it for granted until, alone, the thirst for the presence of other men lights a fever in their bodies and leaves them staggering against the pressure of silence, doggedly fighting their way back to the borders that mark the farthest advance of the feet of men. It is not good for man to be alone; and no one is more conscious of this than the man who has lived without men.

Yet, somehow, loneliness is not necessarily dissipated by the swirling crowds of a city. A stranger in New York walking down Broadway or squeezing into a subway will be bumped, pushed, at least slightly trampled on; but he will feel no gayer for such intimate contact with men. In fact, their very number will serve to emphasize his solitary condition, as a shout of a multitude rushes against the echo of a whisper to drive it back into silence; their closeness will be a yardstick making more vivid the impenetrable distance from the sleeve of a man's coat to the depths of his heart. This lonely stranger is not made less lonely by the crowds any more than a hungry man is made less hungry by the meal that is within sight but out of reach; here there are men in abundance but no companions. His loneliness is not the desperate, panicky thing of a man alone in a desert; but it is a more poignant, deeper, hardly less devastating realization of the insufficiency of solitary man.

Indeed, companions are not the whole answer. Loneliness is a subtle enemy that may slip into the sanctuary of a home and make a desert of it for all the home's luxury and personal propinquity. Perhaps the thing comes about suddenly, with love's explosive expulsion, or gradually through the sad, slow starvation of hearts that want love but not so eagerly as they insist upon convenience and comfort. However it comes about, the day a man realizes he is alone in his home the light goes out of his eyes, the spring out of his step; he is imprisoned in the empty castle of himself and knows himself a prisoner.

Even though he may have the presence of other men, the easy give and take of companionship, and the ready understanding of love, a man has not yet fully armed himself against the unrelenting enemy of loneliness. For the image cannot long substitute for the original, the shadow for the reality, nor the promise for the fulfillment. It is not men nor women nor children that fill to overflowing the empty cup of the human heart; but the God in whose image all are made and whose likeness has been the flickering flame of their desirability, lighting the steps of man who necessarily travels the long road home alone. Once that truth has been seen and embraced, it becomes clear that loneliness is not a matter of empty places, of strange cities, or hollow homes, but of the exile of God.

Obviously, God is not to be exiled. No darkness is deep enough to blind His eyes, no power strong enough to thwart

His might, no life complete enough to stand without His support. He is everywhere, knowing, doing, conserving; loneliness is a sad game of pretense played by the foolish men who try to escape God or the weary men seeking the dark rest of despair.

If the men of our time had their way, God would be on the carpet all the time offering soothing explanations to angry questions. What is He doing in the holes of vice where only bitterness is unrationed? What is He doing in the houses of suffering where a smile is heroic? What is He doing in the broad areas where brutality has found joy in crunching its victims? Are the abandoned, the agonized, the despairing to believe that God is everywhere? All of which means, of course, that we are impatient at God not doing things our way, even angry that He allows men to work out their lives to eternal failure or eternal success. Why does He let men be men; and why does He not do things the way we men would do them, rushing in indignation at the immediate evils that, to our eyes, so patently cry for correction? Strange, paradoxical questions that revile God for the responsibilities of humanity and insult Him for not ruling in the human fashion.

The angry questions cannot change the facts. If there be no God, there is no world nor men to work out their lives in that world; since God there must be, there is no place from which His knowledge, His power, His causative and conserving action can be excluded. God's presence is not won by His knocking patiently at locked doors here and there in the universe; it is not a matter of His rushing madly from place to place, inevitably arriving a little too late; it is a much deeper, constant, intimate actuality than the pervading perfume of incense in a small chapel. The work of man's mind is not to change the fact of God's ubiquity to his own annihilation, but to penetrate its truth to the little degree granted to a mind as feeble as our own.

No point is served by our strolling under the white light of divine truth naively trusting to the hasty make-up of a rationalization to disguise an ugliness we refuse to admit even to ourselves. We find comfort in the divine truths; but comfort that can be relished only by those courageous enough to be honest with God. There is, for instance, the comfort of knowing that the misjudgment of men is a surface storm that can whip up waves destructive of the flimsy structure built along the shores of life, but which can never upset the calm of unsounded depths of a heart that is working primarily, not for the judgment of men, but for the judgment of God. There is the comfort of knowing that the battles of the world are ultimately decided by a judge who really knows the difference between winning and losing, that the fighters who go down, overwhelmed by trampling boots and roaring guns, may well be the winners who would not surrender what could not be taken from them.

There is little comfort here, however, for the enemies who would destroy God in destroying man or destroy man in destroying God. Sin still slinks through darkness in the absurd hope that God will be afraid of the dark or be helpless in it; the hypocrite still practices his amazing sleight of hand, so quick and so expert as to fool himself, stubbornly telling himself that God cannot be backstage penetrating his tricks from the wings, brutality still keeps its eyes so fixed on its cowering victim, that it sees no challenge to its mad power; and deceit still lies glibly, smoothly, smilingly expecting God's memory to be no longer than that of men. God is everywhere, knowing all things: in the lonely reaches that go beyond the law of men, in the howling mob where justice dares not whisper, in the dark strange places where justice is itself a stranger, in the magnificent office where greed is offended by the mention of its name, in the deep recesses of the hearts of men and women, corners to which the light of human knowledge has not penetrated. God is everywhere bringing comforts, yes, but terror too.

For it is not by His knowledge alone that God is everywhere; that fact men might shrug off, once shame had forgotten how to blush. But there is the omnipotence of His power. The modern has seen something of the truth in picturing the ubiquitous omnipotence of God as a refuge for weakness. Certainly, without the certain knowledge of the irresistible power of God, the offspring of weakness among men would be prodigious. In the presence of a superior, merciless power exultantly exercised by their fellows, men know well the twinge of fear, the surge of panic, the surrender of despair; we of today, of all days, know what it is to cringe under the whip, to fly, casting aside all things, careless of everything but escape from a pursuer on fire with hate, to face the barbed wire that does not so much keep prisoners in as it keeps hope out.

But these are only the obvious offspring of physical weakness, born of a high hope that itself is high courage. What of those who do not cringe but surrender, who do not fly but change their colors, who do not despair but simply give up hope? These need no whip, no pursuer, no prison limits, for they have ceased to be men that they might be friends of whatever power dictates the paths men's feet shall walk. Physical weakness, indeed, takes refuge in divine omnipotence; heartened by the certain knowledge of that refuge, physical weakness can refuse to become moral cowardice, until the arms of the headsman tire and blood be too rich a diet for the most savage of men.

It is, in other words, not only weakness but courage that looks to omnipotence; in the ultimate analysis, it is only courage that dares entertain the idea of an omnipotent God. For omnipotence is not something invoked on the enemies who deal out injustice as the merciful deal out bread; it is a divine quality to be reckoned with moment by moment, day by day, as a man casts up the account of his own every action. The weak who look to God must be strong, looking to themselves, for it is not a small thing to stand, undismayed, heart as open as a book, in the living presence of a just and omnipotent God. They are not the strong who blind themselves, while they can, to the surge of divine power that levels the hills and valleys of men's lives; they are the weak, so weak they dare not look over the crest of the hill of today, so frightened they dare not peek around the corner of the moment, so terrified they dare not look facts in the face.

Nor is this weakness bound up exclusively in the men who are the day's instruments of terror. Something of the same thing is contained in the complaints against God which arise from human misery and suffering; men are not strong enough for faith in the divine power, not trusting enough to submit to the plans of Providence, not loving enough to be sure their Father's eternal vision makes a wiser disposal than their own eyes can see.

God is an enemy of the enemies of man and Himself, but, for all that, a kindly enemy. He is present everywhere by His knowledge, His power, and also by that divine action which brings everything real into being and sustains it for its allotted time. Existence, after all, is something proper to God; it is something the rest of the world borrows, in a very small measure, from divinity, not so much cutting off a slice of it as living in the shade of divine existence. God supports all things in being, not taking a man by the arm to help him, not propping him up from behind as though man were a ventriloquist's dummy, not giving him an injection that will enable him to stagger through his days with no more attention. Rather, God conserves all things by being more intimately present to them than they are to themselves. St. Paul made a classic understatement when he said God was not far from any man; indeed He pervades every vestige of reality within, without, and about each man. For unless God be there, nothing real, however minute, however unimportant, or however unessential, could resist for an instant the plunge into oblivion.

Not that we shall meet God if we walk the roads of the world long enough; rather, we shall never escape Him however far we roam, however fast we run, to whatever secret places we slink. Loneliness is a game of pretense; for the essential loneliness is an escape from an inescapable God.

CHAPTER TWENTY-TWO

The Confusing Guest

THE FACT of change is a puzzling guest in human life, taking full possession as though it were one of the household and expected permanent accommodations. Sometimes it looks away from the cradle; then wears such an expression of hope, of joy, of inspiration, promising so full, free and vigorous a life as to carry us out of ourselves. Again, it looks toward the grave; and with such a sober threat that we are frightened, a little panicked, and turn our heads away to escape the gruesome vision. But, then, there may be an excuse for the strange actions of change. We do give it a paradoxical reception. When it is the change that means the beginning of life or life's progress, we greet it joyously, as a kind of personal triumph; when the very same change comes in heralding the end of life, our hearts are torn out of us with sorrow. Birth and death, rejoicing and mourning, bright hopes and gray loneliness: are these two guests, or are they one come unto us under the name of change?

The confusion is really within us, not within change. We are so enraptured of one of its features that we overlook all others; at another time, we are so shaken by its frown as to forget the bright youth of its face that once so enraptured us. The fact is that in every change there is growth and decay; every change is a birth as well as a death; every change, that is, except that intangible advance and succession in the mind of a man or an angel.

In every change that we recognize as growth, there is also decline or decay; something is lost that something else may be gained, something is put off that something else may be put on. Infancy is exchanged for childhood, which is to say that infancy is lost that childhood may be gained; childhood must give way before adolescence can appear; and adolescence, in its turn, decays that maturity may flourish. Maturity is more stubborn, holding its ground for years; then it slowly gives way, fighting inch by inch, insisting the battle is won though all the world can see that old age has carried the day.

The same interplay of gain and loss runs through the activity of every day. Work is hurried through that we may prepare to receive rest in a fitting manner, until rest palls or work calls, and we start a new day by burying the old. One task is finished; and its chief merit is that it has so well prepared the ground for the inception of new work. Old dreams come true and are pushed aside that we may dream again; or they do not come true, yet must make way for new, brighter, surer dreams. Old ways surrender to the new which they have themselves conceived and brought forth, but only by decaying. Old neighborhoods, with their memories of stark beginnings, healthy bustle, refined exclusiveness, slowly sag, crumple, and are abandoned that their pulse may beat on another street.

Only truth and love escape the inevitable combination of growth and decline, birth and death; and often they escape it only a little. For there is often much too much decay of truth that a little of the new may sprout; our hearts are often too crowded with new friends to give breathing space to the old. Facts pour into our minds much too fast to permit of thinking, stifling the old truths and forbidding the growth of new; new interests elbow their way into our hearts and are gone before they can take root and settle down for an eternal growth.

It is true, in a sense, that every day within ourselves we re-enact the drama of the universe. The lamb dies that the wolf may live; from the death of a tree comes warmth and housing for men. Old life has died and bequeathed its ashes; from its grave we bring forth the bright jewels of earth and coal's black jewels of comfort and stored-up energy, as though these were the souvenirs forbidding us to forget that things have lived and died but not without another birth. It is the dying sun that gives life to earth. For every change is a medley of life and death within itself; something dies that something new be born. Something of the substance of mother and father is lost that a child may be born; something physical that is life of their lives, something spiritual that is a death to self and a surrender of consecration. This new life is bone of their bone and flesh of their flesh, a living expression of a unity so great as to demand death to self; in the presence of this symbol of the gallant recklessness of love, selfishness ekes out only a mean, grubby existence, for love will not be forgotten while love's begotten word makes the house echo love's surrender. Through all of life we are in constant rehearsal for the ultimate change to end all change, the change from life to death to life unending.

All change makes a paradoxical demand of motion and stability; something must go, but not everything; something must die but something else must remain to receive new life. The subject of change is moving but in a sense unmoved. It makes for a mosaic of perfection; piece by piece the picture is laid by an artist to whom time means little and the beauty of the whole means everything. Unless one can suffer this agony of patient part-by-part assembly and part-by-part dismemberment, there can be no change.

That element of changeless stability behind change can be read in the human story, but obscurely, mysteriously, between the lines or in the delicate hint of a nuance. There was, for example, the virgin child of Nazareth in Galilee who walked the varying road of human change, from childhood's carefree gaiety through the deep but anxious joys of the wife and mother to the incredibly tragic days of Calvary's sorrow and eventual lonely old age. Yet a note of perfection was sustained through it all, an enduring thing in her own life that made age seem a contradiction, an unceasing thing through the ages that has forbidden men to think of her in terms of anything but vigorous, vibrant, overflowing life; an eternal thing to delight the enthusiastic members of her heavenly court.

Those who have not walked through life blindly have, in their own experience, come face to face with the wisely young and the youthfully old. For into every life there walk those youths who, lacking none of the freshness, vigor, and driving energy which are the proper gifts of their age, have yet an air of stability, of far, clear vision that makes pretense or secrecy seem a flimsy veil to be tossed aside in a kind of surprised relief. In the presence of these, we not only can, we must be ourselves; a little regretfully, perhaps, always a little astonished, and inevitably to the good of our souls. For these have, obviously, a knowledge of men and the souls of men not to be gained by years of knocking about the corners of the world; here we look into eyes alert to read the divine secrets that God has written deep in the hearts of every man and woman.

Just as surely, those who can see have met the physically old who are yet not old. They may move more slowly, be a little bowed by the pack of years they carry on their shoulders; they may prudently save steps, dodge hills, and avoid the extra trip up the stairs that youth takes so blithely. But their eyes deny the shouted tale of old age: alive, a smile in them that almost sports dimples; quick to see, eager to understand, human problems drop all pretense before the saturation of humanity that the years have given these young eyes of the old.

In a more obvious form, this stability in the human story crops up in our grasp of truth. For truth is of the stuff that does not wear thin or threadbare, the furniture of a home that cannot decline with the swift passage of the years. Changes here are only to eliminate the foreign particles (emotion, hastiness, prejudice, error) that cling to it; for truth, the years are a cleaning process that brings out more sharply its fast colors, tightly woven fabric, incredibly complete harmony. As truth gets older in the mind of man, it brings us closer to the stability of the world of things as they are, wiping the film from the mirror of divinity that we may see how closely the old truth in our minds compares with the eternal truth that is behind the truth of the world.

Love may tell some of the story of stability or, again, it may not; for love is an unpredictable story teller born with restless feet and wandering eyes. It may have gathered no more than a wanderer's fortune in its stroll through life: a flimsy hut that a spring shower beats to the ground; a sturdy enough house that is yet not stronger than time. It may even have sauntered just above the layers of clouds, that darken the material world, into a human heart; or it might have climbed to the stars and beyond. It may be a fragile thing, wrapping its arms about loved things that are born to die while in itself, love flares up to a white light, cools off, and grows cold. On the contrary, it may be stronger than the strongest thing on earth, spending its heart extravagantly on the things that die to be born, sustaining that white heat of extravagance, of complete surrender, forever.

It is these last two, truth and love, that give us an inkling of the secret of the ancient young, the youthful ancients, and the unchanging Mother of God. For the first two, the young and the old who are yet not young nor old, have at least embraced truth, the truth of man's humanity, and have loved the things in men that time cannot corrode or coarsen. While Mary was so close to her Son, who is the first truth and source of all truth, she was so intimately associated with infinite love's supreme expression that she was penetrated with the clarity of truth and the warmth of love. To put it in another way, all these people were so close to the changeless One that the perfume of His perfection clings to their garments.

There are two kinds of changelessness. One is the changelessness of oblivion, the unchanging nothingness of that which never was. The other is the changelessness of complete perfection, the changelessnss that forbids growth because it has all, that scorns decline because it can lose nothing. This changeless One cannot be born, for eternally He is; cannot die, for He is life. His is no mosaic perfection, but a single, brilliant, splendid white light that we must break up into its colors to keep from being blinded.

The changelessness, the immutability, of God is no static, repulsively stagnant thing; it is the full story of perfection's ceaselessly intense activity. We recognize the truth of His immutability by the humble salute of respect and love we give to those who mirror it for us: the unchanging Lady of heaven, the youthful ancients and ancient youths, the wise who stand close to the unchanging things of the unchanging One for an eternal view of things as they are; the courageous ones who have not feared to look at the face of truth and take love into their arms.

CHAPTER TWENTY-THREE

Attractive Change

A MODERN formula for a short love story is, with a generous mixture of witty repartee and fast action, to confront a girl with the choice between a completely dependable but utterly colorless boy and his hopelessly unpredictable but incessantly amusing rival. Such a story is as relaxing as the old-fashioned dime novel for, like its predecessor, it puts no strain on the intellect. The plot can hardly be classified as complex. From the very beginning, everyone but the dependable suitor knows he has not a chance; the hopelessness of his suit must be kept secret from him, otherwise there would be no story. Since there must be a story, his rival's claims are persistently toned down by detailed statements of his madcap pranks, his juvenile improvidence and casual thoughtlessness. Time and again he gives the girl abundant reason for terminating the whole affair in justifiable anger; but each offence, brilliant with the flashing lightning of unpredictable variety, only serves to draw her closer to him.

Lest the ultimate choice of this irresponsible moron seem too open a violation of reason, the dependable suitor wears his dependability as a badge of dishonor. A few brown words here and there give him a bilious look that is enough of a prod to the reader's imagination to complete the picture: stodgy, unchanging, boring, monotonous. He plods through the story with a dragging step, his conversation as stiff as sore muscles; his whole character is as settled and solid a thing as dried concrete, so much so that a smile would seem like a sudden jagged crack foreboding tragedy.

Admittedly the girl's choice is one of heart, not head. The readers silently applaud and turn to the next story, never stopping to wonder when or if the playboy will ever grow up; and with never a thought as to what ultimately happens to the stagnant suitor. Presumably he alters his way of life sufficiently to direct his attentions to some other girl, for he pops up again and again in the same role, under a different name of course, but on the trail of the same kind of girl. The applauding readers are not to be sneered at; there must be something sound in the heroine's choice, something universally human, since it does meet with such general approval. Obviously the heroine cannot be the object of mockery without implicating the horde of readers who would have done exactly the same thing. The male characters might well come in for some critical scrutiny as might the author; though it would be well to remember that the author did sell his story and the male characters did sustain an extremely tenuous plot.

The defect in the formula can only be sensed rather than known unless the formula is subjected to a philosophical and theological criticism. And what author armors his stories to withstand fire as heavy as that? The real defect here is that the author did not know enough about time and eternity; hearing such a criticism, he would probably be too astonished to make a gesture of self-defense.

Every reader knows that the male characters were overdrawn: there simply are no men who are so utterly unchangeable as to be stagnant or, if they are, the miasmal character of their lives forbids their being cast in the role of lovers; on the other hand, the utterly unpredictable and thoughtlessly improvident playboy of real life passes from the hands of a nursemaid to those of a guardian or of the police. But the fact is that the author had to overdraw these characters because he was presenting the wrong issue, the wrong problem, a completely impossible dilemma. The girl's choice was not, could not, be between dependability without change and variety without any dependability; it was not the choice between stagnant permanence and unceasing but meaningless change. In the face of such a totally unlikely choice, she would probably settle for spinsterhood.

The basic assumption that gave the story its plausibility and universal appeal was that a man cannot be always the same and not be deficient, for no man can be all things at one time, cannot portray all perfections simultaneously. This assumption is sound, for man lives his life in time, not in eternity; he is human, not divine. The choice, as the story portrayed it, was not between dependability and variety, between permanence and change; it was rather a flight from deficiency, a revulsion from stagnation, to a slight degree of permanence with an immense promise of growth.

What repels our appetite is not permanence but permanence deficiency; what so attracts us is not change, but approach to perfection. At the root of both attractions there is the unquenchable human thirst for the eternally enduring, which is to say, for the completely perfect. It is only the permanent that is perfect which escapes the measuring scrutiny of time.

Time is both a friend and an enemy, a comfort and an agony. It is the measure of the flow of the instant we call "now." Its sovereignty extends over the whole long stretch of the before and after, from the past through the present into the future. Within its kingdom, then, is to be found all the delight of variety, a delight that is soundly based on the recognized limitation or imperfection of anything that can be crowded into this present moment. The parents' eager contemplation of the growth of their child is crowded with this delight of variety, heavy with time: the first tottering step, the first scarcely distinguishable word usher out wonders of the past only to crowd in new wonders of the present; yet the new wonders are just as eagerly surrendered in the delighted contemplation of the masterpiece of the child's first laborious scribbling, its hesitating recognition of words often heard but never before seen.

Variety's delight carries the heart high through youth's impatient rush to come to grips with life; through love's growth, its deepening, to its crescendo of sacrifice; through the almost imperceptible flowering of knowledge and wisdom's slow accumulation. All these belong to time, and time can well be proud of them; they call the heart forth to new adventures regardless of the baggage of the past that must be left behind.

Time is kindly, too, in bringing the relief of escape from the evil of the moment to the peace and goodness of tomorrow. It is a ruthless gunner mowing down the anxious hours by the sick-bed; it speeds on their way the intolerable moments of a night of agony; it brings to an end the prisoner's long years of confinement; and hurries the delightful but tantalizing moments of anticipation. All this time does for us, and we are grateful; for always its favors consist of ushering in yet more of goodness, more of perfection.

Yet in time's territory is included the tragic loss of the precious moments of a good's possession. It is time that takes the bloom from love's full flower, sometimes shriveling it. Time dulls the edge of the intellect's sharp knife to the point where it can no longer cut to the heart of truth. Among its victims are the rush of energy, the dainty fragility of beauty; the swinging stride, the ringing voice, and the hearty laugh of a man in the prime of life. Labor's accomplishments dwindle to a trickle before its icy frown and ultimately stop in frozen terror; it pries loose love's unyielding grip; calls a halt to the dedication of friendship; breaks the forces of power; and stops the pulse of life.

Time is a paradoxical thing that plagues the moments of a man's life. In its merciless arms it embraces all that begins and ends. It claims for its own, and rightly, the alluring mystery of beginnings with all the hope, the love, and the labor that went into them; and, of course, all the long, long roads of adventure which beginnings open up to the human heart and mind, the courage they involve, and the astonished surprise that inevitably greets their success. On the other hand, time no less rightly claims beginnings of quite another sort. To it belong the shock of betrayal, the frightened helplessness against unsuspected injustice, the numbness of loss, the nervousness of new labor, the painful adjustment to poverty or riches, to loneliness or company, to quiet or to clamor. In time's retinue is to be found all the terrible finality of ends. It marks the last surge of accomplishment, the relief of escape, the exhaustion of spent effort, the last agonized gasp of life.

Through time's tollgate must pass all that changes and all that enjoys repose. For a changing thing is a moving thing, and time is the measure of movement. Even though the change be as slow as the gentle rounding of the low, old hills of Ireland by the steady caress of the Atlantic breeze, it must still inch its way through time. Though it may be as fast as light's quick stride across the years from sun to planets, it cannot be fast enough to escape the check-off of time. We are mistaken, however, if we suppose that anything in repose is outside the vigilance of time. It is a terribly serious mistake to confuse rest with eternity. As a matter of fact, it is only the changeable that ever reposes since it is only the changeable that refrains from action or looks forward to action as yet unbegun. The eternal is, then, foreign to repose because it is foreign to change. Our human picture of the work of creation includes a detail of God finishing a laborious job and sitting down to catch His breath and admire His workmanship; but it is a human picture, much more on the side of poetry than of history, for it would put change into the immutable God, withdrawing Him from work, resting Him for future work.

On the contrary, the divine picture of man's eternity is a literal statement of fact that yet surpasses the grandeur of poetry's most sublime efforts; it is the picture of the unending act of man's vision of God, an act that is unchanging, unchangeable, perfectly permanent and permanently perfect, an intense activity that is foreign to repose.

It is not the notion of the absence of all beginning and the absence of all end that is proper to eternity; rather it is the notion of wholeness, of consummate and unimpeded activity, the denial of succession's attempt to escape from imperfection. For it is the permanent that escapes time to be measured by eternity.

As we approach permanence and recede from change, we recede from time and approach eternity. This truth is not a vague, uncertain thing but a certainty upon which daily life proceeds; it is not an esoteric mystery but the casual norm of men of all conditions. So the state takes on an unquestionable importance as it stretches through the length of lifetime after lifetime; it assumes a toweringly terrible importance if men forget the immorality of their own souls, for them the state is the supremely unyielding, unchanging human thing. Constant love wears an air of nobility, it basks in an acknowledged supremacy that dwarfs all other values. Truth wears down the centuries, though it touches the mind of man with only a severely gentle hand, molding it; without comment it states its demands, exacts its sacrifices, lays deep its foundations, fulfills its promises. For all these things recede from change and approach to permanence; they approach the eternal.

In concrete terms, there is the present-day consciousness of the perfume of Mary's sanctity, though it is two thousand years since she walked her quiet way among the still quieter hills of a land tasting the flavors of the quiet that oblivion brings. There is the hard, sharp edge of the doctrine of Thomas still cutting the ragged edges of man's stubborn mind, though it is seven hundred years since he made a holocaust of himself that the flame of truth might burn the brighter. There is the wisdom of the papacy still receiving reluctant tribute from the most cynical of ages.

These things are precious to us, infinitely precious, for they smack of eternity; and the thirst for the eternal is buried deep in our hearts. We try to bring that haunting desire into sharper focus by more clean-cut concepts of eternity, but with indifferent success. Sometimes we picture it in terms of interminable, lopping off the end and the beginning. But that trick can be dangerous, too; the modern world has done it, leaving intact the flowing change of the space between, and come up against a whole hoard of grinning contradictions that it cannot face without embarrassment: contradictions such as a changing world without a beginning, a purposive world without an end, a contingent world without a cause, and so on. As a matter of fact, the lack of beginning or end is entirely accidental to the notion of eternity; to describe eternity in these terms leaves the desription as inadequate as describing a man as a tenor.

On another tack, we conceive eternity in terms of the absence of all succession; eternity is the "now" standing still, like an unceasing moment of ecstatic love, the timeless insight of intuition, the oblivious enticement of concentration. Here we come closer to the true notion of eternity, for this concept unites the notion of intense activity to the note of permanence; yet it leaves a hint of history and a foretaste of change. The most adequate concept of the eternal is that of a simultaneous whole, something like all of a lifetime gathered into one moment by the mind of a dying man, or all of love's expression finding utterance in one word as supreme as the cross on Calvary. For this is the eternal: the utterly permanent, totally unchanging. The notion of eternity follows from unchangeableness as the notion of time follows from movement; the secret of their diverse attraction to the human heart may be seen in the fact that unchangeableness follows from full perfection, while movement is the gesture by which we reach up for just one more perfection that until this time had been desired but not had.

CHAPTER TWENTY-FOUR

Six Ways to be Unhappy

THERE HAS always been a ready sale among men for prescriptions for happiness. The sale is not less brisk in times of world chaos and unspeakable misery; rather, at such times the charlatan, with his utterly improbable wares, does a volume of business that might well be the despair of the philosopher and theologian. Even in normal times, when there is no more than the ordinary quota of misery and unhappiness among men, human hearts are inevitably quickened by the bright promises of a new formula that seemingly puts happiness within easy reach of hands that have too long grasped for it in vain.

The ready reception given to the self-appointed apostle of happiness is revelatory of some of that paradoxical mixture of strength and weakness of men that makes them an eternal puzzle, an eternal exasperation, and an eternally unpredictable attraction to other men and, if we may speak of divinity in the human fashion, even to God. There is a common note in every prescription for happiness; in every one men see a bright, young allure and a solid looking promise of quick, tangible results. Not that the author of the latest formula has found a better model, brighter colors, or a more original technique; the radiant beauty and assuring confidence do not spring from the formula for happiness so much as from the unquenchable and resilient courage of the heart of man. The eager response to a promise that has so often failed is itself an unshakable testimony to the constancy of the vision that is hope and the effort that is the child of that strange human courage which will not admit defeat.

Yet, at the same time, the fact that there is always room for a new prescription for happiness quite reasonably gives rise to the suspicion that perhaps it is hard work to be happy, work too hard to be sustained for all the years of a lifetime against the unrelenting attacks of time and sorrow. The fact is that all these new prescriptions flourish for a time because they make happiness look so easy; and, without exception, they inevitably pall because they do not produce the one result they promised. Yet the old prescriptions that have weathered the ages are deserted again and again with a discouraging promptness because they make no secret of the labor involved in scaling the heights of human living. In normal times a superficial observer might even suspect that many people do not want to be to happy because they are reluctant to leave themselves without the material for a single grumble. But in times such as these, times far from normal, such suspicion is surely unjustified.

Along with their common notes of attractiveness and easy results, these continually appearing formulas for happiness unite in a universal deficiency; none gives the complete happiness promised to the eager hearts that so joyfully embraces them. Still, this thing of happiness seems so simple in itself: apparently all that is necessary is to point the heart at a goal and then let fly with life. It is, of course, important that the goal be the right goal and that the aim be steady, not wavering. But neither of these essential conditions seems to be a highly complex demand. Perhaps we have made the right answer to the question of happiness a little too simple. Men have been swindled so often trying to purchase happiness that now they are darkly suspicious of what seems to be simple and sure. Moreover, it is a not unpleasant human quirk to make our accomplishments look particularly difficult; in this way, people are impressed, and we have too few opportunities to impress people, and we ourselves are furnished with an antidote against all the discouragement of abandoned projects and evident failures.

If we went at the matter of happiness in a more complex manner, perhaps men would see it as satisfyingly simple. Instead of asking and trying to answer the question of how one can be happy, perhaps we should ask how can one be unhappy, and then proceed to do the opposite. At least the experiment is worth trying.

It is to be understood, of course, that a merely plausible course to unhappiness will not satisfy our present quest; we are looking for the short, direct route. There is no room here for patience with nostrums of unhappiness; the object here is to uncover means that are absolutely guaranteed to make a man unhappy. From that point of view, ruling out all half-measures, there are just six ways in which a man can be sure of making himself unhappy and, with a reasonable amount of apostolic effort, of bestowing a certain amount of misery on those who come into contact with him. The secret of the first four ways lies in the careful choice of starting points or premises; the fifth is a much more violent, and very well known, method that hinges on the choice of a goal; while the sixth demands a certain slithery dexterity in technique.

The first guaranteed method of unhappiness may be called the method of the cynic or the method of the whiner. It is not surprising that a choice of title is offered for this first method because after all, the cynic is really a whiner whose tears come out in snarls. Briefly this method consists in basing one's life solidly on the premise that nothing in life gives any happiness whatever. With that premise laid down and sedulously maintained, the system is foolproof, misery is assured, and there will be no shortage of snarls or tears. By this method the heart is made to droop in unceasing self-pity, and absolutely nothing in the world or in men can distract it from its dark contemplation.

The second method makes a tramp of the heart. It consists in maintaining, despite the disillusion of experience and the history of all the centuries of men and women who have left their testimony on the matter, that something in life gives *perfect* happiness. Adopting this system of unhappiness, a man can be sure of many a strange adventure on many a dark road with the guaranty that every road will bring him to his goal of un-happiness, absolutely none of them will trap him into happiness. He will have a busy, vagrant life, sopping with disappointments; if he remains loyal to this system to the very end, his heart will eventually attain to a state of frowziness to be expected in an aged hobo. The natural temptation to the devotee of this method of unhappiness is to slip back, somewhere shortly after middle age, into the first method; this temptation can, however, be pro-vided against by an earnest cultivation of an extreme giddiness or by setting life to such a pace that in time a man cannot stop. In this latter case, the happiness involved in the hope of the rest of a goal is thus successfully avoided.

The third method for unhappiness is not too difficult, though it demands an absolute concentration on the present moment; if that concentration is interrupted for even a few moments, the whole system crashes and unhappiness may slip through one's fingers. On the whole, this method is a rather imaginative sort of thing; it demands that life's premise be a picture of happiness tied up in the minute bundles that make up the moments of every day. The only one to be sure of is the one that has been delivered to your door just now; that package must be grabbed up instantly, ripped open and devoured before it is taken away. The technique here is to squeeze the maximum amount of fun out of every minute; its goal is to pile up a total that will surpass all other totals. A man who adopts this system need never fear an incursion of happiness; his misery is certain, for he can never be sure of the balance of fun outweighing the burden of misery until he is dead—and then, of course, he will not mind. This system makes a glutton out of the human heart and sets it to eating so greedily that it cannot taste the food. As a guaranty of unhappiness, this leaves little to be desired.

The last of these methods whose secret lies in their premises is undoubtedly the easiest of the lot. The only effort it demands of a man in return for its guaranty of unhappiness is the de-velopment of a degree of timidity, the more the better; it simply will not work well unless a man learns to be afraid of almost everything. But with that condition fulfilled, it rolls down a smooth road to uninterrupted unhappiness. The premise it lays down is that complete loyalty must never be given to anyone or anything. By this system a man develops the technique of embracing with one arm, letting the other hang free just in case anything attractive comes along. Following it industriously, a man learns to love with great caution, alertly looking over the shoulder of his present love for other possibilities. In this way, you see, he is continually thinking beyond and behind the present to its complete neglect. As the past is gone, the future has not come yet, and he is three-quarters blind to the present, his unhappiness is completely assured. As he progresses in this system, he will discover himself becoming thoroughly lukewarm, not quite giving up anything, never quite attaining anything. His heart will spend all of its time teetering on the fence; not unusually it will be a barbed-wire fence.

The fifth guaranteed method of unhappiness is extremely simple, and millions of men can vouch for its complete effectiveness. By this system a man has only to aim his life at the wrong goal to be sure of unhappiness. Lest the simplicity of it gall a man's pride, a variety is offered in the choice of wrong goals. Really, though, it makes little difference whether a man choose a goal beneath him (say in terms of the cosmic, the animal, the social, or the humanitarian), on the same plane through a divinization of hero-worship, or within himself; in each case the fundamental guaranty of unhappiness is the same and for the same reason. For the sake of unity, this fifth method could easily be put in the same classification as the first four since it, too, has a fundamental premise. It supposes, as essential to its method, that a man starts out convinced that human beings are not human. But obviously such a dose would be much too bitter for the intellect to swallow if offered as the first nourishment toward unhappiness; the method is put over more effectively if it is couched in vague terms, preferably with a certain air of nobility, learning, or common sense. The delightful thing, to the gourmand of unhappiness, about this method is that the misery it brings comes all at once, with a smashing, climatic effect that surpasses anything the other systems have to offer;

it is not until the very end, until the goal itself is reached, that a man can know the full, exquisite bitterness of despair that has been prepared for him through all his years of effort.

The final absolutely sure method of unhappiness is, in a sense, disappointing. It has little of the finality, the catastrophic character, of the other methods. All it can be certain of accomplishing is to torture a man with alternating jabs of despair at what he has lost and frustrated desire at what he must give up. This method demands that a man take wavering aim at the right goal: when he misses it altogether by mortal sin, he will be in despair or at least will be seized by terrible fright; when he hits it by virtuous action, he will still be tormented by the forbidden delights of sin. The system is not satisfactory from the point of view of unhappiness, for it allows happiness to creep in again and again in the moments of repentance.

Taken all in all, these six methods are close to sure ways to unhappiness. If there is one common element in them, then, there we can locate one of the great impediments to happiness. A very little study will uncover the fact that one of the very great attractions of all six methods is the permission they give a man to hold fast to the small, tangible things that make such a vivid appeal to him. Their common weakness is that, enabling a man to hold to the little things, they force him to loosen his hold on the big things. The great impediment to happiness, then, is our human reluctance to part with what we willingly admit are trifles: little pleasures, little conveniences. Of course, any rival attraction is small compared with the goodness of the Last End, who is God; but here the question is really one of trifles, the trifles that stifle the human heart.

It is quite impossible to formulate six methods for hapiness to rival these six for unhappiness; for, you see, there is only one way for a man to be happy. In contrast to the demands of the six systems for unhappiness, a general prescription for happiness would include such as these: the courage to want to be happy; an expectance of continual and increasing but always imperfect happiness as life winds to a close, for life is a way, not a home; an unwavering aim, at the right goal. Translated into the terms of the supernatural life which man must live to be happy, this prescription for happiness would include:—the courage to love the Cross; the expectance of a full share of sorrow and an imperfect but increasing happiness as we approach closer to God; the direction of our life to Him; with complete loyalty to the directions of His commands.

It is, however, hard to be happy; but not nearly so hard since the Son of God came to dwell among us, leaving us His Mother and Himself to be with us all days. With Him so close, happiness is not far off; without Him, unhappiness is upon us.

CHAPTER TWENTY-FIVE

Sudden Interest

IT WOULD be difficult, in these days, to tune in on any radio station for any length of time without hearing indignant denunciations of attacks on the rights of man, tragically told accounts of offenses against human dignity, and invitations to join a crusade in defense of the sacred sovereignty of the human individual. This comes as a little shock to older listeners. They remember such things as the evolutionary vogue that made men a moment in a process without beginning, end, or meaning; the slave conditions of early industry in the liberal countries; and the contemptuous dismissal of the poor in the era of "natural law" ethics. Young listeners are even more bewildered. They have just come from universities where most of their days were loaded with the charge that the human individual is not only insignificant, he is a worthless victim of illusions: without a purpose in life, without a mind capable of truth, without morals of any lasting value, without a will committing him to responsibility.

All in all, a good many years have been spent trying to convince free men that they are small potatoes indeed. Now there is a sudden about-face. It seems John Doe is important after all; so important that all nations must respect, honor, and labor for him while the world revolves around his destiny. It is all very flattering, but why has he become so terribly important? Is anyone really convinced of it? Is it, by any remote chance, true? If it is, John Doe should rightly demand a terrible reckoning of this last century for its colossal deception of him.

The totalitarian claims to interest in and respect for the human individual have been made more than suspect by official counterclaims from the same sources; the facts have made this alleged interest preposterous. From the side of the democracies, the facts have been kinder, conflicting counterclaims have been reassuringly absent; but the reasons given for human dignity and its claims to respect are anything but heartening. Thus, for instance, a university sponsored round-table discussion on a national network featured four nationally prominent men who agreed, as to a basic assumption, that man had inviolable rights because the state gave them to him.

Indeed, the whole argument, as adduced by the most vocal of the modern democrats, is reducible to something like this: the human individual is tremendously important, of sovereign dignity, because we like to feel that way about him or because the state has taken that attitude toward him.

No penetrating intellect is necessary to perceive that importance and dignity on such grounds are frail things indeed. Perhaps we shall not feel that way about man tomorrow, or perhaps the state will take a contrary attitude next week. The man in the street is quite sure of his individual importance. Before he goes at the business of making radical sacrifices for a government, however, he would like to be certain that the government and its leaders are just as sure as he is, and on the same solid grounds.

This average man is no adept at dodging or mutilating facts; he is satisfied to take the facts as he finds them and face their full meaning. He knows that he resents, and reasonably so, any attempt to push him about. He is affronted by the attempt to make a tool or an instrument of him, though he takes it for granted that all else in the universe should be put to work for man. In other words, he sees clearly, though he may never put it into such words, that the individual man is worthy of respect, that he has inviolable dignity and a sovereignty which all else must serve because he is the only creature in the universe *who cannot be used.*

Physically, of course, the thing is possible; it has been done from the beginning. But whenever and wherever, a man has been used, he has been abused, and his abuser has been debased.

Men and women have been used by dope peddlers, by white slavers and their customers, by pornographic theatrical producers and their clients; and both the abuse of the victims and the debasement of the aggressors have been too patent to be questioned. It is not less true that the correlatives of abuse and double debasement have put in their inevitable appearance when human beings were made mere tools of the owners of sweat-shops and of factories that escape that name only because of their size; of agricultural overlords; of military conquerors; or political schemers. As a matter of fact, even benevolent despots, smiling their smile of paternal patience and thoughtfulness while they treat men and women as children, have always abused men and debased themselves.

All these cases, with which human history so tragically abounds, are radically the same. In all of them a human individual has been abused: his mind, his heart, his action have been frustrated; his life reduced to despair. In all these cases, the abuser has been debased, for in every case he has been put either in the absurd position of a comic-opera divinity or of a ruthless tyrant. No man can be a tryant until he is first tyrannized by greed, pride, power, or some other of the vices, with a total loss of appreciation of his own human value; until, in other words, he has abandoned his claim to respect on the grounds of humantiy. No man can play at God until he has first entertained a genuine contempt for humanity, even for his own humanity.

Such results of the use of man are inevitable. For man, alone in the physical universe, was not made to be used but to use all else. He is not a slave but a master. His immortal soul outlasts the world; his vision pierces the future and the past; he is master of his every act and is responsible for every moment of all his days. He deserves respect. He has his own high dignity. He is a sovereign being. These are things that belong to a superior; and man is superior in the universe *because he is the only spiritual thing in it.* He can use all else precisely because he is spiritual; he cannot be used by anything else precisely because he is spiritual, with an end of his own transcending the purposes of every other created thing.

There are human rights, in other words, because man is man, not a moment in a process, not a worthless victim of illusions, not the spoiled favorite of a state, or the beneficiary of a social attitude. On purely natural grounds, man cannot be abused without nature's terrible penalties being incurred. When it is remembered, as it is so seldom remembered today, that man has been adopted into the family of God, the full desecration of the abuse of man stands out in all its unholy viciousness. With this desecration there can be no comprise, no program of appeasement, no thought of surrender.

CHAPTER TWENTY-SIX

A New Virtue

A NEW virtue has been discovered in America. It has been glorified in best sellers, canonized by official usage, made to feel at home in the crowded family of the virtues. No doubt America should feel proud of this latest achievement of its pioneering genius; this is the first addition to the family of virtues in the history of men.

Obviously, it is no easier to discover a new virtue than it is to discover a new sin; and centuries of sinning have introduced no new variety into the devil's garden. This seems quite as it should be, for, after all, the principles of man's sins have not changed, nor have God, men, or angels—the only objects of his sins—undergone any alteration. On much the same grounds, it might be argued that there is no possibility of increase in the family of virtues; but that is to reckon without the modern mind.

We have found a brand-new virtue and christened it Tolerance. Of course it has some resemblance to the older, somewhat worn virtues. It is, for example, not unlike that distinctively Christian courage that goes by the name of patience. In fact, if tolerance meant to tolerate, it would really be the same old patience under a new name; for then its routine work would be putting up with nuisances, while its full perfection would consist in bearing hardship and sorrow without letting grief flood the soul to the point of complete surrender. Tolerance, in this sense, would mean that extraordinary strength which is capable of sustaining a terrific beating without suffering defeat.

This new virtue, however, does not deal primarily with nuisances, hardships, and sorrow. It embraces opinion, error, truth, good, and evil. It tolerates all opinions on all but scientific subjects; it tolerates all religious beliefs and all denials of religious beliefs; varying shades of stable moral codes and the denial of all stable moral codes; philosophical and theological truths and the denial of philosophical and theological truths. Clearly it is not patience but a much wider virtue carrying with it a surer guaranty against conflict of any kind. Patience endures evil because this evil can be met only by endurance; there is no kindly feeling in the heart of patience for the evil afflicting it. It girds its loins for a dogged fight that is necessarily defensive, prepared to take the beating that cannot be escaped. Tolerance, on the other hand, is on the best of terms with everyone and everything; its particular attraction is that it avoids any threat of a thrashing.

Its good humor makes it look something like Christian charity. It should not, of course, engage in hearty laughter; for laughter is a decidely definite commitment to one point of view that might be offensive to another. But it can and does smile ceaselessly, almost woodenly as proof of its universally kind feeling. It strikes no blows against anyone or anything. It will have peace at any price. It excludes no one or no thing. The doors of its heart are as open as an unfenced field. Within its hospitably spacious tent the lamb and the lion can lie down together, or the lion can eat the lamb, or, for that matter, the lamb can eat the lion. Tolerance will make no trouble about the whole thing one way or another; it cannot make trouble, for, though not all things to all men, it is the same thing to all men.

Yet the differences from charity are striking enough to warrant this new virtue's claim to novelty. Paul could say that the charity of Christ urged him on; it is hard to picture tolerance urging a man on, particularly to such things as Paul faced: to hunger, thirst, imprisonment, scourgings, and death.

Charity encompasses all things by renouncing them all to embrace their source; tolerance only smiles at them all, including their source, with its frozen, tolerant smile. Charity hates evil, destests sin, fights to its very last breath that sin may not conquer. Tolerance is no fighter, and above all no hater. Which is to say, that tolerance is no lover. When we have said that much, we have perhaps said all that need be said about tolerance.

The tremendous staying power of patience is accounted for by its high estimate of the good which its refuses to relinquish whatever the punishment it must undergo. Charity's intense drive, unquestioning sacrifice, and fighting loyalty are not at all mysterious; for charity is love. On the other hand, it is extremely difficult to determine what makes the wheels of tolerance go. The puzzle, perhaps, is really not so much what makes the wheels of tolerance go, but rather what paralyzes them in inaction.

For tolerance does not, in fact, do anything, embrace anyone, champion any issue. It wipes the notes off the score of life and replaces them with one long bar of rest. It does not attack error, it does not champion truth, it does not hate evil, it does not love good; and if anything else be said of its action, it must be said negatively, denying all action. This very fact solves the difficulty of the mainspring of tolerance; for a man is dedicated to inaction only by a lack of interest that sees nothing worth the difficulty of moving toward it. If it is insisted that tolerance is a virtue, it must be defined as a habit of doing nothing from a conviction that nothing matters.

Actually, tolerance includes a serious contempt of men in its boredom with all values. It is not kindness to smile on the sins of men, though it is charity to smile on the sinners as one fights the sin; it is not thoughtfulness for men that smiles on their championship of error, though it is charity to embrace the erring while you slay the errors; it is not love of men that inspires an equally pallid welcome to atheism, paganism, and divine religion; it is contempt of the very things that matter most in the lives of men, and so contempt of the men themselves.

Tolerance is the twentieth-century substitute for the charity of Christ, but this contemptuous tolerance is a far cry from Christ's loving toleration. There is much to be said for the toleration of men and women whatever they may have believed, said, done, or planned to do; so much, indeed, that the Son of Mary will accept no quibbling excuses for the lack of it when the last questions are asked. Such toleration includes a fighting opposition to all that threatens the image of God in men and the attainment of God by men. It is not the product of that supine indifference which bears the name of tolerance today the indifference that finds nothing important enough to warrant a struggle, not even men.

THE "WHY" OF LUMEN BOOKS

For a long time we have considered the question—"Why do Catholic books in general—even those with popular appeal—have such a relatively low sale among Catholic people?"

We feel that the secular press has given us the answer to that question. POCKET-SIZE BOOKS—with slick and attractive covers, sturdy bindings, and a very low cost seem to fit the modern tempo. The price is right and the size is right. (The contents, however, are another matter!)

Pocket editions have had a phenomenal appeal and sale. We feel that their success in the secular field (225,000,000 copies in 1949) has demonstrated the need for low-priced reading. Most Catholic families simply cannot afford the cost of an extensive library.

However, Catholic publishers are not usually wealthy organizations, and for many good reasons they have not gone too deeply into the field. But NOW the time has come to invest in an experiment on behalf of Christian reading. The result of our experiment is found in LUMEN BOOKS.

LUMEN BOOKS is an attempt to put good literature into the pocket book field. Distribution will be made at the parish level, in the church vestibule, the school, by direct mail, by the book dealer, and by organizations interested in the development of good reading taste.

Lumen Titles are for You—

June releases:

The Least of the Brethren By Harold J. Heagney.

An absorbing life of the great Dominican saint, Martin de Porres. Anyone who has read Father Heagney's books, *Seven Came to Judge, Madame de Chantal,* his serials in *Extension,* and his many other works, know him to be one of the most fascinating Catholic writers. This book is a *must* for the Catholic reader.

Title No. 518, 50¢ postpaid.

Come With Me to Mass By James V. Linden, S.J.

One of the best written accounts of the Mass, step-by-step, ever published. Father Linden, Regent of Law at Gonzaga University, tells the story of the Mass to a non-Catholic friend. The book is simple— anyone of average intelligence can understand it. It should be part of every Convert Class, and every Catholic should read it.

Title No. 517, 50¢ postpaid.

Fiction titles soon to be released:
The Hallowed Hour, A. H. Parr.

This is one of two books written by the industrialist who gave up his business to engage in real Catholic Action in the field of literature and motion pictures. He found that he had great talent for writing, and turned it to the production of novels embodying Christian principles. *The Hallowed Hour* is a gripping story of Christian love.

Title No. 516, 50¢ postpaid.

The Mountains Moved is another of Mr. Parr's moving stories of great faith. Packed full of adventure and action, its realism points up the great moral which he brings to his readers.

Title No. 515, 50¢ postpaid.

LUMEN Best Sellers:

The Looking Glass By Walter Farrell, O.P.

A fascinating book of reflections for women by the Dominican scholar who wrote *The Companion to the Summa.* Father Farrell's style, sometimes whimsical—and always interesting and easy to read, brings his points straight to the mark.

Title No. 514, 50¢ postpaid.

The Family for Families By Francis L. Filas, S.J.

This fine book, originally selling for $2.50, is written by a pioneer Cana director. It is the application of the intimate family life of Jesus, Mary and Joseph to modern, married living. With original art work, foreword, and study club outline.

Title No. 513, 50¢ postpaid.

In Garments All Red By Godfrey Poage, C.P., life of St. Maria Goretti. Sixteen pages of photographs, with maps. In second printing.

Title No. 511, 50¢ postpaid.

The Red Lily By William D. Ryan.

The Children's life of Maria Goretti, a LUMEN "Junior Edition." Lavishly illustrated with photos, maps, songs.

Title No. 512, only 25¢ postpaid.

Order from your Bookstore or direct from

Lumen Books—A Paluch Publication

P.O. Box 3386   Chicago 54, Illinois